THE ULTIMATE GUIDE:

Genuine And Innovative Ways

To Make $100 Dollars

A Day Online

TOM OWENS

All rights reserved.

No part of this book may be reproduced, stored in any retrieval system or transmitted in any form or by any means of photocopying, electronic, mechanical, recording or otherwise without the permission of the author and publisher

Copyright©2022 Tom Owens

TABLE OF CONTENT

INTRODUCTION 8

CHAPTER ONE 12

PAID SURVEYS 12

    When To Stay Away From An Overview Site 25

    Ways to bring in The Most Cash In Taking surveys 26

    Best Practice for Taking Paid Internet based Overviews 27

    Things To Know About While Taking Paid Online Surveys 29

CHAPTER TWO 32

FREELANCE WRITING: BECOMING A FREELANCE WORDPRESS DEVELOPER 32

    What Is Freelancing? 32

    Freelancing As A Profession 33

    Reasons to become a freelance WordPress developer: 34

    Some Of The Best Freelance Marketplace Websites Right Now 35

    Becoming A Freelancer In 7 Easy Steps 37

    Getting Freelancing Jobs 44

    Taking Care Of Your Finances 46

CHAPTER THREE 50

SPONSORED BLOG POSTS 50

    What Is a Sponsored Blog Post? 50

    A Prologue To Sponsored Blog Posts 52

    How to get sponsored blog posts (6 key tips) 53

    Advantages And Disadvantages Of Supported Blog Entries: 56

    What You Need Before You Get Started (Checklist) 58

How Much Should You Charge For Sponsored Posts? 59
Factors to Consider Before Accepting Sponsored Posts 60
    What you need to look out for in a sponsor: A Sponsor's Fit for Your Blog and Audience 60
    How to Get Started With Sponsored Posts (Step-by-Step) 64
    Three Tips for Writing Sponsored Posts 68

CHAPTER FOUR 74

AFFILIATE MARKETING 74

What is affiliate marketing? 74
    How to get started with affiliate marketing 75
    How Does Affiliate Marketing Work? 84

Types of Affiliate Marketing 86
    How Do Affiliate Marketers Get Paid? 88
    Why Be an Affiliate Marketer? 90
    Common Types of Affiliate Marketing Channels 91
    Benefits to Joining the Big Commerce Affiliate Program 94
    How to Join The Big Commerce Affiliate Program 95
    Tips to Help You Become A Successful Affiliate Marketer 97

CHAPTER FIVE 102

WORKING AS A VIRTUAL ASSISTANT (VA) 102

    What do Virtual Assistants do? 102
    Common Tasks Of A Virtual Assistant 102
    What amount do Virtual Assistants Procure Each Hour? 104
    What do a virtual assistants Make Each Year? 104
    Bringing In Cash As A Virtual Assistants 104
    How to Get Started With Your Virtual Assistant Business 106

Step by step instructions to Amplify Your Income from virtual assistant Occupations *108*

CHAPTER SIX 110

SELL PHYSICAL PRODUCTS ONLINE 110

How To Get Started *110*

CHAPTER SEVEN 120

CREATE ONLINE COURSES 120

Pros and cons of creating online courses *121*

How to Create an Online Course *123*

CHAPER EIGHT 128

LAUNCHING A PODCAST 128

Motivations to send off a Podcast: *129*

Guidelines to Begin a Digital recording: All that You Want to Be aware to Succe *129*

The disrepute of digital recordings *130*

Step By Step Directions To Start A Computerized Recording *130*

How to present your digital recor podcast to Spotify *145*

How to present your podcast to Apple Digital broadcasts *145*

CHAPTER NINE 150

SELL DIGITAL PRODUCTS ON GUMROAD 150

Reasons to sell advanced items on Gumroad: *150*

Method To Procure A Side Pay Selling Digital Products *151*

What Is A Digital Product? *152*

Advantages of Selling Digital Products *153*

Some of the Best Digital Products to Sell Online *155*

Digital Product Ideas *158*

Platforms to Help You Sell Digital Products Effectively *160*

CHAPTER TEN..**164**

    OTHER BUSINESS IDEAS AND INDUSTRIES THAT ARE THRIVING AND WILL THRIVE **164**

CONCLUSION

The Ultimate Guide

INTRODUCTION

The web is a spot loaded with business open doors and thoughts for online side gigs. You don't need to spend a little fortune to begin an internet based business and start bringing in cash. You simply have to do all necessary investigation, track down a thought that suits your abilities and way of life, and play it brilliant. A large portion of the internet based business thoughts referenced below allow you the opportunity to fire little and scale up once you make serious areas of strength for a personality. Keep in mind: supported web-based achievement takes time, which is the reason persistence, is a critical temperance for all business people.

In the event that you're a teenager, odds are your day to day plan is now really loaded up with school, extracurricular, family commitments, and, obviously, your public activity. Yet, who says you can't bring in additional cash as an afterthought? Independent composing is a pleasant method for utilizing your abilities and interesting point of view to bring in cash. Being a consultant permits you to deal with your own timetable, and you can decide to take on so much or as little work as you like. Many organizations and online distributions are energetic for new, youthful voices, and there are large number of various specialties you can compose for.

One more incredible method for bringing in cash as a youngster is through paid surveys. Albeit this isn't precisely a customary, consistent pay, it tends to be worthwhile and possibly even tomfoolery. Organizations and counseling firms put a ton of time and cash into realizing what youthful purchasers are keen on - and who would have zero desire to get compensated only for imparting their insight?

Its a well known fact that one of the principal abilities most students get in highschool and school is the capacity to compose expressively and engagingly on a wide assortment of points. All in all, why not utilize these abilities to bring in some additional cash in the meantime? Filling in as an freelancer is an extraordinary method for making additional money as an understudy. Albeit the sum you procure will change in view of the site you're composing for, the kind of satisfied you're composing, and how long you put in, freelancibg can be a great method for bringing in cash while fostering your remarkable tone and composing style. Do you feel like you're prepared to change from student to master? In the event that you've fostered your insight and involvement with your specific field enough, it very well may be an ideal opportunity to make your own web-based course about it. With the fame of online courses expanding consistently, this moment is an extraordinary opportunity to reach out and share your insight. I referenced a couple of extraordinary hotspots for making and selling your web-based course.

You've collected an abundance of involvement all through your life - why not share it with others? Quite possibly of the most ideal way you can procure an additional pay as a senior resident is by utilizing your expert, creative, or educational encounters and distributing a digital book. One more fantastic method for bringing in cash online as a senior is to function as a menial helper. Being a VA may not be ideal for everybody, since you will frequently must be dealing with your boss' timetable as opposed to your own. Be that as it may, in the event that this isn't an issue for you, then being a VA can be a low-stress method for procuring a pay from home utilizing your PC and relationship building abilities.

Going further into this book will expand your viewpoints and thoughts and try out ahead in sticking to a specific business

CHAPTER ONE
PAID SURVEYS

One direct web-based side gig for you to bring in income sans work is doing paid surveys. Did you have any idea that there are bunches of sites out there that offer you to take surveys and afterward pay you for them?, Without a doubt, it's not the most productive endeavor, however it merits offering it a chance since it's so natural and accessible. Assuming that you're stressed over the authenticity of this sort of pay, don't be. Paid surveys are totally genuine and they're utilized by huge number of organizations out there.

Organizations need suppositions from clients and purchasers to work on their items and administrations, as well as to make new ones, and the web permits them to contact individuals who can furnish them with dependable information, individuals in any case wouldn't get the opportunity to reach. Indeed, that is where you come in. A paid surveys is fundamentally offering your perspective on a help or item and getting compensated for it! You should simply join (free of charge!) on a paid internet based survey website and begin earning in cash! In any case, be careful about spam destinations that request that you pay to utilize their overviews.

Taking paid surveys online is a simple assignment you can do to bring in cash in your extra time. Overview organizations work with organizations that need criticism about groundbreaking thoughts or items before they hit the market. Study takers make money for addressing questions that will assist brands with working on their items. Finishing up reviews for money can merit your time in the event that you pursue the right overview locales and execute a couple of supportive tips. All you want is a internet connection and a PC or cell phone to get everything rolling.

Looking for the best web-based overviews for cash, here are the most ideal choices out there that will pay you to take studies for cash;

1. Swag Bucks

Swagbucks is one of the most paid surveys site claimed and worked by Prodege, LLC. Maybe the most famous study site on the planet, it holds a 4.4 rating on the Application store with 61,000+ surveys, and a 4.2 rating on Google Play with 84,000 extra audits. Finished overviews pay somewhere in the range of 1 and 350 Swagbucks (additionally called SBs), contingent upon the length and point fame. For each 100 SBs, you'll acquire an extra $1 that can be recovered for PayPal money or gift cards to places as Lowe Amazon's, and Target. New Swagbucks individuals will get a $10 information exchange reward in the wake of expenditure no less than $25 at one of the site's highlighted retailers like Amazon, Best Purchase, or Walmart. Paid online surveys are not by any means the only method for bringing in cash with Swagbucks. The organization grants its individuals SBs to shop on the web, search the web, and watch recordings. You can begin recovering your profit when you arrive at 160 places. In three days of latently utilizing the stage, I gathered 256 focuses — generally comparable to $2.56. More than thirty days with a comparative exertion, I'd hope to procure around $25. The more SBs you amass, the higher the worth of the gift cards you can recover. You can open more store choices and find gift vouchers to places like Starbucks, Walmart, and iTunes. Swagbucks is a well known review site that will pay you to take overviews. As you take reviews, you'll procure Swagbuck focuses which can be recovered for money or gift vouchers. You can likewise acquire Swagbucks focuses for such exercises as messing around, looking through the web and watching recordings.

You can hope to procure around 40 to 200 Swagbucks for each review. That winds up between 40 pennies and $2 per study. Nonetheless, there are a few intriguing chances to procure up to $50 per study. This is seemingly the most well known paid review site on the planet.

2. Survey Junkie

This is one of the simplest, most clear survey sites on the web. It's a free enrollment site where you can procure up to $50 per survey. You'll get your most memorable paid review offer when you join and you can take it when you're prepared. Survey Junkie has an A+ rating with the Better Business Department and a huge number of individuals around the world. Survey Junkie permits you to bring in cash by taking reviews and sharing your perusing conduct. As you answer reviews, you will aggregate focuses. Inside your dashboard, you can see precisely how much the focuses are worth in dollars.

You can reclaim your focuses for cash by means of PayPal or gift cards. The main disadvantage is that you should hold on until you gather 500 focuses to cash out at the $5 mark.

3. InboxDollars

The incredible thing about InboxDollars is that it doesn't rehearse the point framework - it works by offering you cash immediately (through PayPal, yet additionally, assuming you need, through gift cards). You can bring in cash by taking studies, watching recordings, and reading messages, yet in addition by purchasing from chosen stores. The reviews on to $20, and each survey requires 2-25 minutes of your time, contingent upon its length. InboxDollars offers you $5 assuming you hint up with them. InboxDollars has been doing business starting around 2006 and was procured by Prodege, LLC back in 2019. They hold A-rating with the BBB. As per its site, the organization has paid more than $80 million to its individuals. InboxDollars clients gather profit in real money rather than focuses, which makes it simple to realize the amount you'll procure prior to focusing on an errand. Most paid open doors offer a modest quantity of cash, yet the more surveys you take, the more you can procure.

It's allowed to join and get everything rolling with InboxDollars, and you will get a $5 reward once you initiate your record. You'll then respond to a couple of straightforward inquiries concerning your pay, race, schooling, and other segment data. This underlying screening will assist InboxDollars with coordinating you with pertinent paid surveys. InboxDollars rewards clients for steady everyday use with cash rewards (on top of typical gathered income). Alternate ways you can bring in cash with InboxDollars incorporate watching video promotions, and shopping on the web at stores like Objective, Walmart, and eBay. I acquired simple pennies playing the games presently accessible for north of 30 minutes however got $1.50 taking the paid studies accessible to me subsequent to enrolling (get more familiar with the involvement with our InboxDollars survey).

4. Branded Surveys:

Branded Surveys holds a 4.3 out of 5-star rating with Trustpilot with north of 48,000 client surveys. The parent organization, Marked Exploration, has been directing statistical surveying beginning around 2012. Whenever you register as another part, you'll procure 50 focuses, then, at that point, one more 50 focuses will be credited to your record in the wake of finishing up your profile (a $1 join reward altogether). Clients procure 50 focuses ($0.50) for finishing the enlistment interaction and 50 extra focuses for finishing the initial poll. When your record is made, you can quickly begin taking overviews, which can be worth up to $5 each. After you arrive at 1,000 places (equivalent to $10 USD), you can trade out your profit out your nearby cash (USD, computer aided design, GBP).

Branded Surveys dedication program, Marked Tip top, offers the chance for anybody to procure extra focuses consistently. You can expand your reward sum by progressing through Bronze, Silver, and Gold levels. To propel, you should finish a specific number of endorsed surveys, and your reward depends on your identification level. I procured $7.41 and almost arrived at the Silver identification level inside the initial 2 hours of utilizing the stage. Dependability levels permit clients to gather focuses at a higher rate prompting higher hourly income. Extra ways of gathering Marked Study focuses incorporate welcoming companions to join, taking the everyday survey, positioning on the competitor list, and being haphazardly chosen for up to 1,000 places.

5. Toluna:

Toluna is a paid review site that works with huge brands like Coca-Cola, Amazon, Kellog's, L'Oreal, SONY Music, Fiat, and some more. It's exceptionally appealing on the grounds that it permits you to pick subjects you like so you can have a good time doing the reviews. You can get installment from them in real money or through vouchers. Likewise, they as of late presented their games area, which permits you to mess around and bring in cash!

Toluna Influnencers allows you to pick the points you might want to take reviews. Albeit this might make the stage really fascinating, the installment potential open doors aren't simply great. For each study, you will acquire somewhere in the range of 15 and 50,000 places. You may not see the focuses credited to your record for a few days. Sadly, your focuses will lapse subsequent to being in your record for a very long time. With that, it's critical to spend your focuses moderately rapidly. As you reclaim focuses, you will actually want to browse cash by means of PayPal and a few gift voucher choices.

6. Opinion Outpost:

To get compensated to take studies with Opinion Outpost, you should finish the underlying screening. You'll need to address inquiries concerning things like your schooling level, work status, and the quantity of kids you have. Then you'll finish a survey in light of ongoing occasions like whether you've taken your pet to the vet or watched a film in theaters. Opinion Outpost will ask duplicatsamens en route to ensure you're noting sincerely. Most surveys are worth 3 to 30 places. You can cash out with the expectation of complimentary Amazon gift vouchers or $10 iTunes or Application Store gift vouchers, or a $10 PayPal credit. On the other hand, at 30 focuses you can open games on Alawar.com or join the Mileage Plus Program to utilize your focuses toward movement credits. You'll require something like 105 focuses to get 300 Honor Miles. Opinion Outpost offers the absolute most lucrative studies we've found. I as of late finished a shopping and retail study and procured $2.50 in less than 30 minutes. The greatest con we've found is that the quantity of studies clients are qualified for is lower than that of other paid online survey destinations we've utilized. Learn more as we would see it Station survey.

On a humanitarian note, consistently Opinion Outpost makes a gift to the American Red Cross to pay tribute to the time its clients take to finish reviews. Its corporate gift doesn't influence your focuses balance, yet you can utilize your focuses to make a different gift in the event that you'd like.

7. Ipsos I-Say

Ipsos I-Say is an overview site situated in Paris, yet it permits clients all over the planet to get compensated to take reviews. It has an A+ rating with the Better Business Department and a 4.0-star rating on Google Play with more than 88,000 surveys. You can enroll with Ipsos I-Say by making a record utilizing either your email address or Facebook account. You'll then respond to a few segment questions so the organization can interface you to important open doors. For instance, in the event that you're another mother, you might see a study getting some information about which diapers you use. After you complete a review, you'll procure focuses. The amount you acquire differs, however it's commonplace to procure between 45 to 90 focuses per review, or $0.45 to $0.90. You can likewise procure up to five focuses on the off chance that you're precluded from taking a review. When you arrive at 500 places, you can cash out your desires for PayPal cash, gift vouchers, or altruistic gifts.

I-Say offers you paid overviews through IPSOS, a statistical surveying firm. I-Say doesn't contain as large of an assortment of paid reviews as different destinations on this rundown, yet it's as yet a generally excellent site you can bring in additional money from. It works by the focuses framework, yet you can constantly recover your focuses either for money or gift vouchers.

I-Say interfaces clients with overview open doors through Ipsos, which is a statistical surveying firm. Despite the fact that you won't have as many study valuable open doors, you will not need to explore another site each time you take an overview. As you develop focuses, you can reclaim them for gift vouchers and money. Awkwardly, I-Say doesn't give a money worth to its places. All things considered, you'll need to look at the accessible recoveries at an opportunity to score the best arrangement. You should stand by 96 hours from your enlistment before you can begin changing out remunerations.

8. LifePoints

Initially known as Public Family Assessment, LifePoints has been around starting around 1946 and has in excess of 5 million individuals all over the planet. Trustpilot gives the organization a 3.9 out of 5-star rating in light of 13,000 genuine part surveys. You can turn into a part free of charge and begin procuring LifePoints by taking web-based overviews. You'll get a prompt 10 LifePoints added to your record when you confirm your email address and give fundamental data like your name, date of birth, and address. Finishing up a total profile will permit you to see and choose overviews that fit your segment.

LifePoints review points range from innovation to cars, to family brands, and then some. Some studies pay up to 600 focuses, or $5 each, however most open doors pay somewhere in the range of $0.50 and $1 to finish. We share more about the paid open doors with the organization in our LifePoints survey.

9. Pinecone Research

Following 21 years in business, Pinecone Exploration has procured a spot among probably the most elevated evaluated paid surveys locales. Pinecone Exploration is claimed by The Nielsen Organization, which holds a rating of A+ with the BBB. Pinecone Research individuals impact future items and administrations each time they complete an internet based study. Each study pays 300 focuses, worth $3, and ought to require a couple of moments, as per the organization.

You can likewise get compensated to test new items as an individual from Pinecone Exploration. You'll be paid somewhere in the range of $3 and $5 to finish a short report on every item. You could try and be permitted to keep the item after the review is finished. Pinecone Research is one of the more world class study destinations and limits its individuals in light of socioeconomics. You can apply so that participation might be able to check whether you qualify.

10. Overview Addict

Overview Addict is one more forerunner in the study business, with a BBB rating of B. The organization has been doing business starting around 2011 and serves in excess of 10 million individuals.

Overview Addict is most popular for the essentials and chiefly offers paid review open doors. This site tracks profit as focuses. Each 100 focuses equivalent $1 procured, and it takes at least 1,000 focuses (or $10) to cash out by means of PayPal or with e-gift vouchers. The website offers a clients the opportunity to bring in cash testing items, partaking in on the web or in-person center gatherings, or by means of telephone studies. It pays somewhere in the range of $5 and $150 per task, yet that choice is very restricted right now.

Begin bringing in cash in no less than five minutes when you join and complete your profile. A large portion of the overviews are genuinely simple to finish. You likewise will not be compelled to pursue something or purchase anything to finish a study. Our main thing about the stage is that they grant you an ostensible number of focuses regardless of whether you're excluded from a review. You might acquire everything showed, except it's worse than no profit from your time, just like with numerous other review destinations.

11. American Customer opinion

American Customer opinion (ACOP) is claimed by Choice Expert, Inc. which has been doing business for over 41 years. The BBB gives this site an A+ rating. At the point when you pursue a record with ACOP, you can begin your most memorable paid review in less than two minutes. Your most memorable overview pays five focuses and incorporates questions with respect to your segment data like conjugal status and training level. Assuming there are reviews accessible, you will see them recorded in your record. ACOP keeps things straightforward and offers just overviews for cash. The organization amasses your profit in focuses, and you'll have to procure 1,000 focuses, or $10, to cash out.

12. Panda Research

Panda Exploration has paid out more than $2.2 million to its individuals starting around 2005. The organization is claimed by A&A Promoting, Inc. what's more, has a B+ rating with the BBB. To get everything rolling, you'll have to finish your part profile and affirm your email address. The organization likewise requires a substantial telephone number to turn into a part. Then, at that point, you can take studies that settle up to $50 each. You can likewise procure up to $25 per time you cash out for perusing paid messages.

Panda Exploration pays individuals with profit of something like $50 on the first and fifteenth of every month by means of PayPal. Note that you will just accept your installments in additions of $50, so assuming you have all out profit of $110, you will actually want to cash out $100 and the surplus will extend to a future installment demand.

13. Survey Club

Survey Club has been around starting around 2005 and has an A+ rating with the BBB. On the off chance that you join as a part, you'll join in excess of 16 million different clients. After you become a part and give your segment data, Survey Club will interface you with paid surveys. It additionally eludes individuals to different destinations like Survey Addict, LifePoints, and Pinecone Exploration. Your profit from reviews facilitated by Overview Club are added to your record in real money, and you can cash out when you acquire no less than $25.

Survey Club likewise gives paid center gathering open doors. It reports the typical income of the people who take an interest as $50 to $200 each hour.

14. MyPoints

MyPoints, claimed by Prodege, LLC, has been doing business starting around 1996, holds A rating with the BBB, and has paid out more than $236 million to its 10 million individuals.

With MyPoints, you can take online surveys for cash, however the webpage additionally has other paid gigs. These incorporate shopping on the web and available, printing and reclaiming coupons, watching recordings, messing around, and booking travel facilities. It likewise gives you five focuses on the off chance that you are not able to take a review, with a limit of 25 preclusion focuses each day.

All of your profit through MyPoints collect in focuses. You can guarantee a $3 gift voucher once your record arrives at 480 places. Or on the other hand for 15,800 places, you can get a $500 gift voucher.

Note that focuses may extend further relying upon where you recover them. Recovering focuses for a prepaid Visa card requires at least 1,500 and is worth 150 focuses per dollar, or $10. MyPoints gives $10 Amazon or Visa gift vouchers to new clients. You'll have to burn through $20 or seriously utilizing MyPoints shopping to reclaim this reward.

15. PrizeRebel

Since its presentation in 2007, PrizeRebel has paid more than $19 million to its 9 million individuals. PrizeRebel's information exchange process rushes to finish. You simply have to give your name and email address. Subsequent to affirming your email address, you can begin taking paid internet based studies. The principal required study requests your segment data and is worth 10 focuses. You can cash out when you've acquired somewhere around 500 focuses, worth $5. Most studies pay somewhere in the range of 40 and 60 places and can require as long as 15 minutes to finish.

PrizeRebel has an exceptional program that grants individuals in view of the degree of profit. On the off chance that you procure 4,500 focuses, you'll arrive at Gold level status and get a 1% reward on your income and a 1% markdown on your award. The platinum level (10,000 focuses) gets you a 2% reward and a 2% rebate, and the Precious stone level (16,000 focuses) gets you a 3% reward and a 3% markdown.

16. KashKick

Notwithstanding surveys, KashKick pays clients for watching recordings, riding the web, and pursuing arrangements through the stage. Surveys are comparable to industry guidelines, with chances to acquire upwards of $2 per finished survey. Installments are handled like clockwork, and you really want somewhere around $10 before you can cash out through PayPal. The essential grumbling from previous clients is losing profit to idleness. Assuming you neglect to confirm your email address, give inaccurate contact data, or don't sign into your record for 60 days, your record may be deactivated. For this situation, any income you had will be relinquished.

You can reactivate your record in no less than 6 months, however you can't get back any past profit. KashKick cleaned idle records just prior to handling installments, so make certain to sign in routinely and check your email address so you don't lose your prizes.

17. Valued Opinions

Established in 2004, Esteemed Conclusions is a statistical surveying board with north of 3 million individuals expressing impressions on items for significant brands like Amazon and Target.

To join Esteemed Conclusions, you really want to finish an enrollment structure utilizing either an email address or your Facebook account. You'll then, at that point, get an email with a connection to snap to initiate your record. To fit the bill for their paid internet based studies, you'll have to respond to extra inquiries regarding your socioeconomics. In the event that you have any life altering events, similar to a move or adding a pet to your family, try to refresh your profile to get more chances to partake in overviews.

Valued Opinions pay clients in real money; there are no focuses to track or change over completely to dollars. Each study is worth between $1 to $5. When you reach $10, you can cash out your income for gift vouchers.

18. OneOpinion

OneOpinion is claimed by advertising research firm Dynata, which has been doing business beginning around 2002 and has an A+ rating with the BBB.

You can begin by enrolling for a free record. In the wake of finishing the enlistment cycle, you'll get an email affirmation. From that point onward, you can start acquiring focuses by taking overviews you fit the bill for. Most reviews are worth 500 to 1,000 places, yet you could discover some that are worth more. When you arrive at the base limit of 25,000 places, you can cash out for e-gift card, actual gift cards, or PayPal cash.

When To Stay Away From An Overview Site

Albeit the locales on our rundown are dependable, you can't confide in each site that professes to pay you to take overviews. Stay away from study locales if they:

- **Request installment;**

A real overview site won't ever request that you pay to join.

- **Request private data forthright;**

you ought not be approached to give your Federal retirement aide number except if you've acquired no less than $600.

- **Have no history or ratings**

Deep rooted organizations are more reliable. You can peruse what genuine clients need to say regarding them and check their set of experiences of installments and accessible open doors.

- **Pay too little**

. Real organizations will have a few more lucrative open doors worth finishing.

- **Have a glitchy or outdated site**

Organizations that don't deal with their sites may not deal with their individuals.

- **Make it hard to qualify for surveys.**

Try not to squander energy on an organization on the off chance that it reliably precludes you for studies.

Regardless of whether the site appears to be genuine, on the off chance that you have one or two misgivings about it or it spams you with messages, eliminate yourself from its rundown. There are sufficient quality study pursuing open doors accessible that you can keep away from ones that disturb you or are certainly not a solid match.

Ways to bring in The Most Cash In Taking surveys

There are a few things you can do to expand your profit while taking studies for cash.

Stick with a few trusted sites. You don't have to sign up with hundreds of survey sites to earn some cash. Focus on the best, highest-paying options.

Fill out your profile completely. Completing your personal profile on each survey site allows the company to match you with relevant offers. Update your profile if you have a life change, like having a baby, getting a pet, or quitting smoking. You might find yourself eligible for new or different surveys.

Watch the time. Keep track of the time spent completing surveys. You're not likely to earn a high hourly rate completing easy surveys so, if possible, do surveys when you have small windows of time, like when you're standing in line to fill a prescription or waiting for a meeting to start.

Answer consistently. Take the time to read each question and respond honestly and consistently across sites. Survey sites compare answers and can disqualify users who appear to be inconsistent in their responses.

Check for free offers. Some survey sites have a "free offers" section where you can earn points for signing up for free trials or newsletters. You can also watch for exclusive bonus opportunities on social media and refer friends to your favorite sites to earn free money or bonus points.

Take the highest-paying surveys first. If you register with multiple websites, you might receive dozens of surveys to choose from. Take a few minutes to estimate your earnings per hour before you start a survey. You may be able to make more by picking the highest-paying opportunities first.

Best Practice for Taking Paid Internet based Overviews

Regardless of whether an overview site is dependable, there are still insurances you ought to take.

1. **Use a different email address**

Making a different email address for overview offers will keep your work and individual inboxes clear of messiness. Besides, assuming that you quit doing reviews, you can quit browsing that email account as opposed to withdrawing from a lot of locales.

2.   **Be aware of what you share**

Great study organizations will stay quiet about your character. Yet, that doesn't make it protected to furnish them with your Federal retirement aide number, driver's permit number, or ledger numbers. Real review organizations needn't bother with this data.

3.   **Use enemy of malware programming**

Hostile to malware programming can keep your PC infection free. On the off chance that you visit various study destinations each day, it's critical to shield your PC from noxious spyware and infections.

4.   **Take regular breaks**

Finishing overviews can be drawn-out. Enjoy regular reprieves from your screen so that you're not enticed to hurry through overviews and give off-base or conflicting responses.

5.   **Fees and bogus commitments.**

Any survey site that commitments you'll procure thousands every month is either a trick or if nothing else deceiving. Ensure the destinations you join offer reasonable expressions about your possible profit and how much time it takes to finish studies.

Paid online surveys are the ideal side gig for somebody searching for a simple gig to do while at home or in a hurry. If you're awkward sharing your segment data or have any desire to procure a high hourly rate, you ought to think about an alternate choice. In any case, to check online studies out, be reasonable about the amount you'll make. Deal with your time shrewdly so you augment your income, join with different destinations to get the best open doors, and exploration the organization prior to enrolling.

While there are better ways of bringing in cash on the web, most will require more ability, preparing, and time than taking reviews for cash.

Things To Know About While Taking Paid Online Surveys

Before you plunge into the universe of taking web-based overviews for cash, remember these pearls of insight:

- **Never pay to take online overviews**

In the event that you are approached to pay to join a study webpage, run for the slopes. You've probably found one of the many tricks prowling in the web-based review space. Shopping at a genuine retailer through these locales is OK, yet paying a participation expense of any sort is a warning.

- **It can take more time than you naturally suspect:**

Not exclusively will it require investment to fabricate your focuses, it can likewise require extra investment to accept your remuneration. You could have to stand by days or weeks to see the prizes you legitimately acquired. Sadly, this is by all accounts a typical subject across survey locales.

The Ultimate Guide

CHAPTER TWO

FREELANCE WRITING: BECOMING A FREELANCE WORDPRESS DEVELOPER

What Is Freelancing?

Freelancing is an agreement based profession where rather than being enlisted in an association, the individual purposes his abilities and experience to offer types of assistance to various clients. In basic terms, outsourcing is the point at which you utilize your abilities, training, and experience to work with different clients and take on different tasks without focusing on a solitary boss. The quantity of tasks or undertakings that you can bring simply reduces to your capacity to follow through on them as asked from them.

Freelancing for the most part includes occupations (called gigs) that permit you to work from home. However, don't relate Freelancing as equivalent to having a work-from-home work.

- Freelancing doesn't by and large suggest that you'll work from home. You could have to work at your client's office depending on the sort of work and the client's essentials.

- A work-from-home occupation incorporates an understanding among you and a singular business who gives you a remuneration while Freelancing doesn't.

It is essentially huge quantities of the places that experts perform can be passed on over the Internet without their participation at the association or client's place.

A Freelancer or free worker is a freely utilized person who gets cash by offering kinds of help to various clients. These administrations connect with the individual's abilities and are not really given to simply organizations. Freelancer either use safe stages like Fiverr, 99designs, etc to get business or use their association to directly get more business and propose sorts of help to their clients. Regardless, is it a good choice for a work? Might you anytime at any point support a rich life while Freelancing? How might you start with Freelancing position?

In light of everything, when 11% of the working adult people in the US is working fundamentally as full-time Freelancer, there ought to be something to be grateful for about this industry.

Freelancing As A Profession

The climb of experts has achieved the improvement of another thought - the gig economy. In the gig economy, an individual, as opposed to working for a lone supervisor full-time and getting a proper pay thusly, works for various clients in light of his circumstances and at an expense, he thinks his work merits.

Freelancing is a attractive profession it manages essentially all of the issues of a standard assist. As per Upwork, Americans work a normal of 47 hours of the week. Freelancers work a normal of 11 hours less each week than full-time utilized laborers. That amounts to around 550 hours of the year or 23 entire days. Full-time Freelancers spend right around an additional whole month consistently behind the control center (or any spot they work). This close by benefits like an open door to work from wherever during a time of your choice, being your own boss, keeping all of the advantages, and a lower cost of working certainly attracts a numerous people to take Outsourcing as a calling. In any case, not very many breeze up seeking after it full-time.

Nowadays, a steadily expanding number of associations and affiliations comprehend that not having an online presence in the 21st century basically moves toward implosion. Regardless, generally couple of business visionaries and bosses have the specific data that preparation and running an exquisite and utilitarian site requires. This is where you step in. Considering that you're a refined web engineer, you can start a site design studio work in WordPress objections. Why just WordPress areas? Without a doubt, simply considering the way that WordPress is a CMS (content organization structure) that powers 43% of the web.

In spite of the way that there's a monstrous collection of speedy WordPress subjects and free WordPress modules, numerous associations and affiliations search for capable help to re-try their areas. If placing assets into reliable web working with isn't an opportunities for you yet, you can offer your administration on free business community locales like Upwork, Fiverr, and PeoplePerHour.

Reasons to become a freelance WordPress developer:

- 43% of all locales are WordPress-controlled, the importance is you'll have a wide goal market;

- freelancing licenses you to pick your endeavors by your schedule and work from home;

- freelancing is a phenomenal strategy for building your portfolio and work on your abilities.

In case you have solid abilities to make and can quickly get the hang of many different places in a short proportion of time, then, you should endeavor independent compositions. Dependent upon the work, the amount of words, and the client's spending plan, you can make less and more than $100 every day. Some word count necessities are under 500 words, but most of them are commonly some place in the scope of 1,200 and 2,000 words.

Nowadays, there are a great deal of destinations you can search for free work. It would be ideal for you to just join and survey your capacities and ability. A part of the regions could demand an current portfolio.

Some Of The Best Freelance Marketplace Websites Right Now

Upwork

On the off chance that you've at any point fiddled with freelancing, you must've caught wind of Upwork, a webpage that extends to various types of independent employment opportunities in areas like IT, programming, and website architecture, as well as visual depiction, composing, interpretation, designing, and engineering. It's an extraordinary spot to look for independent work on the off chance that you're simply beginning.

Contently

As the name recommends, this organization is pointed explicitly at independent authors. Contently works by interfacing authors with top worldwide brands. To pursue their administrations, you should upload a portfolio, so this is suggested for additional accomplished essayists who have many finished projects and essentially a couple of years of work insight added to their repertoire.

We Work Remotely

This is one more incredible site to look for freelancing jobs. It extends to distant employment opportunities from one side of the planet to the other, for a wide range of tech and composing skill.

Freelancing

This is an older platform; many laid out specialists initially began on freelancing.

Fiverr

It extends to an extensive variety of outsourcing position, among which you can track down loads of composition and interpretation gigs too.

freelancing offers a unimaginable chance to control the way that you work. As a freeelancer, you have the opportunity to work from anyplace, whenever. Engaging advantages like these are prompting the development of the freeelancig business. More than 33% of the U.S, truth be told. labor force is at present freelancing in some limit, as per Upwork's new Freelance research study.

Yet, how would you begin as a freelancer? If you have any desire to venture out towards turning into a consultant yet doesn't know how to start, you're perfectly positioned.

Popular Freelancing Occupations

Clients are looking for productive experts to handle their interests across basically every industry, work, and scope of capacities. Regardless of what your occupation is like, a client is looking for an expert like you to handle their anxiety. Coming up next are irrefutably the most notable freelancing position:

- software developer
- Graphic designer
- Web engineer
- Writer

- Digital marketer

A large number of associations use Upwork's work business focus to track down gifted experts considering more than 5,000 capacities and 100+ groupings of work. In excess of 10,000 autonomous entryways are posted on Upwork consistently.

Becoming A Freelancer In 7 Easy Steps

Why might you want to transform into a freelancer? Is freelancing an additional income source, a chance to expand your work knowledge, or a replacement for your standard work?

freelancing offers the chance of choice. There are different ways of advancing for freelancing. You can begin your journey in your additional time or push toward it as a full-time profession. Regardless of your strategy, the seven phases recorded underneath will guide you past countless the ordinary hindrances that new experts face.

1. Define your administration and offering

Transforming your abilities into a help is the initial step to turning into a consultant. To do this, you'll have to comprehend how your abilities can help an imminent client. Attempt to place yourself in the shoes of your optimal client. What issues do they have, and how might your abilities be utilized to determine the issue?

It's fundamental to perceive that clients are searching for an answer for an issue. To be a fruitful consultant, you really want to comprehend what is going on and utilize your administration to resolve their issue. The solution to these inquiries will be the underpinning of how you bundle your abilities as a help. Presently it is the ideal time to think of a concise depiction of the assistance that assists you with offering your independent help to organizations.

Attempt to compactly make sense of what you can do, how you get it done, and for what kind of business/client. Try not to stress over the cost at this point; we'll get to that as we advanceadvances.

2. Find your main interest group

Since you bring an independent support of the table, you'll have to track down a main interest group. Begin by distinguishing the sort of clients that will be ideal for your administration. Do these clients have a common issue and normal qualities? Is it true or not that they are in a particular industry?

As another consultant, simply being perfect at what you do isn't sufficient to naturally have clients searching you out. It's pivotal to situate yourself before your possible clients so they can find out about your administrations. You'll have to play a functioning job in tracking down likely clients. For most specialists, there are three methods for securing clients:

- freelancing posting forums

- Influence existing associations and systems administration

- Marketing, advertising, and outreach

Understanding which of these choices turns out best for you is critical to tracking down important clients for your administrations. "I began my independent business on Upwork in 2020 and tracked down my freelance client through Upwork's foundation. Over the course of the past year, I have developed my business only through Upwork and client references without paying for promoting or going to a systems administration occasion.".

Upwork is a work commercial center that helps specialists and clients interface and participate in significant work projects. On Upwork, clients are effectively posting accessible undertakings across various classes and addressing top cost for quality work. You can look through here to track down projects that match your abilities.

3. **Develop a price structure**

When you have obviously characterized your administration and your objective market, now is the right time to set your cost. The objective is to amplify the sum you're paid without missing out on possible positions. Thus, begin by checking out at your rivals on the lookout. What are they charging for comparable outsourcing administrations?

As a general rule, there is no ideal equation for evaluating your specialist administrations. Numerous factors can influence the sum that clients will actually want to pay:

- Experience

- Industry

- Project term

- Expectations

- Project complexity

- Client's geographic area

- urgency

Luckily, Upwork has a few valuable assets to assist you with exploring how to price your freelancing administrations. For more data, look at the two significant estimating models that specialists use: hourly pricing and project-based (fixed) evaluating.

Try not to let vulnerability about your pricing structure hold you back from beginning. Your rates are not long-lasting. You can transform them later on. Begin with a cost you feel OK with and do whatever it takes not to over think it.

4.   Create your portfolio with past positions

Making a convincing portfolio is a vital stage to turning into a fruitful freelancer. As a freelancer, your portfolio lays out your work quality by displaying your achievements and past undertakings. This is your chance to show and not just simply telling clients what you can do and the worth of your ability.

Your portfolio ought to feature your best business related to your administration offering. Each piece in your portfolio ought to illustrate your commitments and how that project helped the client. A portion of the things that a solid portfolio could incorporate are contextual investigations, tributes, information driven results, pictures, graphs, work tests, and models. It's essential to get consent from your past clients prior to integrating their undertaking materials into your portfolio.

5.   Write an incredible proposition

To guarantee a fruitful beginning as a consultant, your most memorable task ought to intently match your work insight and capacities. At the point when you find an undertaking that you're certain that you can offer fantastic support for, now is the ideal time to present a proposition. The right proposition can mean the distinction between getting some work or not, so having a recommendation that works for you is basic.

On Upwork, presenting a task proposition is simple and direct. Utilizing locales or stages other than Upwork, you can in any case use this proposition construction to show your worth to possible clients. So, a legitimate proposition ought to be serious areas of strength for a point for your capacities. It requirements to frame the organization's necessities, how you can help, and give your accreditations and capabilities. At last, staying proficient and well disposed is critical, so attempt to utilize proficient language to assist you with sticking out.

Making a layout can assist you with sorting out your proposition, yet the best specialists tailor it to the particular client and venture. Taking that extra forthcoming time and exertion shows your truthfulness, excitement, and impressive skill.

6. **Create a rapport with your client**

As a freelancer, your clients are your company. While it might appear glaringly evident, fostering a positive working relationship with your clients is significant. Effective specialists lay out associations with clients as opposed to considering the work a limited time offer arrangement. Building a drawn out organization can prompt recurrent business and new client references. Here are a few central issues to remember while making a relationship with your clients:

• **Accomplish amazing work:** Top notch work is vital for client fulfillment. You really want to offer some benefit and tackle the client's concern to get an opportunity to construct a drawn out relationship with the client.

- **converse with the client**: Compelling client correspondence makes a more grounded business relationship and urges clients to keep on working with you for future undertakings.

- **Fabricate trust through transparency:** By reliably finishing your work on time and giving precise expectations, you can construct trust and demonstrate the way that your client can rely upon you later on.

- **Track down amazing chances to offer more benefit:** By stepping up, recognizing new arrangements, and taking on extra obligations, you exhibit your expected worth to the client and open up better approaches to cooperate.

7. **Keep fostering your abilities**

freelancer are recruited for the help and abilities that they proposition to their clients. Therefore, it's a critical for specialists to reliably work on their abilities, adjust to changes, and grow their insight. Staying aware of latest things is likewise fundamental to giving your clients the most noteworthy help level. Internet learning assets like Udemy, LinkedIn Learning, Coursera, and even YouTube are incredible beginning stages for guaranteeing that your abilities are dependably updated. Why, you inquire? All things considered, the response is fundamentally implanted in our human mind. It is well established in our psyches to search for an assurance. A standard occupation furnishes us with an assurance of a calling that pays at the predefined time. You get a daily schedule to follow. What's more, this occupation additionally gives ensured advantages, for example, protection, retirement benefits, opportune asset, augmentations and pay climbs for performing great.

At the point when you decide on outsourcing, you lose the assurance of any of this. There's no guarantee that you'll get repeating clients. No guarantee that you'll have the option to support this way of life till retirement, and, surprisingly, no assurance that your pay will at any point increase.

In addition, you get to deal with your expense derivations, protection, and different funds yourself.

There are additionally different other cons to freelancing

- **Balance between work and personal life:** On the off chance that you don't have the foggiest idea how to isolate individual life from work, outsourcing becomes harder than an ordinary regular work.

- **No compensation:** Specialists are responsible for their own days off, days off, get-aways and should be great monetary and time-usage organizers.

- **Difficult Clients**: You might discover a few clients who are incredibly hard to make due. They might bomb in giving the right directions and data for finishing the task or might be difficult to reach to clear any questions. This can be baffling and could bring about burning through your time.

There are generally upsides and downsides to each occupation and it ultimately depends on you to adjust it appropriately for a solid balance. In the event that you think freelancing could be useful for yourself and the cons don't make any difference much. Peruse on to figure out how you can turn into a freelancer.

Getting Freelancing Jobs

Turning into a freelancer is similarly basically as simple as requesting something over the Web. You visit locales that proposition independent positions and errands and take them on. This is a superb approach to beginning and getting your name out there.

The following are a couple of locales that you can pursue outsourcing position:

- **Fiverr:** the world's peak business place to look for autonomous positions. Basically make a record post what you can do, add several connections, and you're done.

- **99Designs:** An optimal spot to get freelancing positions if you're a fashioner.

- **Upwork:** Upwork is a more master looking free business place where you'll find more business clients.

- **Freelancer.com:** Freelancer.com is among the most settled autonomous work business focus which you can pick in your basic year when you have essentially zero autonomous experience.

We have a complete examination of best reevaluating destinations here to check extra decisions out. Managing several gigs from these regions helps in understanding how rethinking as an undertaking comes and helps you with getting its hang.

Notwithstanding, before going to these free destinations, you need to set up an autonomous brand for yourself. Follow these methods for something almost identical;

- Finish up what administration you'll offer.

- Choose your goal market.

- Find the stages (reevaluating destinations) you'll serve on. Pick a uniform username on all of them. It helps you with building your picture character.

- decide on your rates.

- Make a web put together portfolio with respect to your specialty unequivocal portfolio stages; GitHub for engineers, Behance for fashioners, etc. We moreover suggest you make a singular portfolio site to show off your capacities and capacity.

- Market your administrations: market through electronic amusement, offer something in vain or at a very low cost.

We don't propose you leave your ongoing sort of income and bob into rethinking basically. Endeavor it as a parttime challenge to see how it shows up for you in the hidden months. It is by and large unreasonable that you want to be independent full-time. It relies upon you to choose whether you should do it full-time or keep your ongoing work and make a buck during your additional energy. Assuming you feel that you like freelancing, this present time is the best opportunity to forge ahead toward the ensuing stage and acquire cash re-appropriating.

Resultant stage

At the point when you feel that you can oblige yourself and work thusly, the accompanying system is to take on various assignments for various floods of pay. This should integrate gigs that you got explicitly using the techniques referred to above as well as from the reevaluating objections.

One more opportunity is that you could make it a full-time gig. Freelancing full-time also infers you can make arranged kinds of pay. You can:

- Wrangle month to month retainers

- Orchestrate commissions on bargained projects

- Make reference systems to remunerate clients who send you new clients

- Market yourself clear: Here's a helpful helper on exhibiting and making ideal individual checking for yourself.

Taking Care Of Your Finances

While in a task, a large portion of the "cash stuff" is dealt with by your employer. You get a customary check without asking; your charges are deducted naturally, and protection is probable likewise dealt with by your manager.

The situation are different when you're all alone and you'd need to deal with the accompanying without help from anyone else:

- Getting your Check: This is viewed as the trickiest part to handle, be it for the outsourcing veterans or the novices. Arranging and discussing appropriately with your client to inspire them to pay for your administration at the predefined time ends up being a very remarkable test. Deal with this appropriately and you are all around set to do perfect in the freelancing field. Look at this aide on negotiating like a pro to assist you with acquiring tips and knowledge.

- **Charges:** You want to deal with your individual and professional tax intricacies yourself.

- **Insurance and retirement benefits:** You want to search for the best protection contract and plan for your retirement yourself.

All that really matters is that being a consultant and working in the gig economy implies getting a sense of ownership with your own funds, whether negotiating your compensation, tracking down protection, or paying taxes. Yet, assuming you love the opportunity, adaptability, and procuring likely that accompanies being autonomous, then freelancing is a very smart idea.

Conclusively, freelancing is an equilibrium of positive and negative. You essentially have to pick assuming you're compelled confronting the test that regularly goes with it. freelancing suggests capable open door, but it similarly infers flimsiness and the bet of disillusionment. Likewise, that may not be what you truly need in your master life. However, if you risk your solidarity for something different in accordance with your master targets than a standard work, you get the opportunity to develop your name and reputation and show up at your master goals.

CHAPTER THREE
SPONSORED BLOG POSTS

What Is a Sponsored Blog Post?

A sponsored post is what content blog proprietors distribute for the benefit of a business trying to get their content, item, or administrations before a group of designated readers. It's really been around for more than 100 years, beginning with radio soap operas.

Radio broadcasts made sequential projects that recounted stories like the present crime podcast. Delivering that content was costly, so radio broadcasts moved toward family products organizations for sponsorships. Procter and Gamble was quick to make it happen, and in light of the fact that they promoted their clothing detergent during these radio broadcasts, they became known as "soap operas." In the current variation, the supported blog section can take many designs, including:

- Posts formed by the support and dispersed on your blog.

- Posts that are made by the blog owner noticing rules given by the support.

- Backlinks to a help's webpage or content that is added to your blog.

- product reviews or giveaways dispersed on your blog.

- Rundown of a brand's suggestion.

- A gathering that consolidates the supporters product.

- An item statement that integrates a markdown for blog perusers.

The following are two or three instances of supported blog entries:

sponsored content may likewise allude to web-online entertainment messages, pictures, info graphics, videos, and more. Yet, we will concentrate on supported blog post. A supported post, by and large, is the point at which a brand or organization pays a blogger to distribute content that includes an item or service. Supported content is a shared benefit for both you and the organization that pays for the sponsorship. You bring in cash and the organization gets its item or service before new audience your blog readers.

Sponsored posts are understandable. Fundamentally, companies and organizations pay you to compose great stuff about them (their services and their products) on your webpage or blog. What you really want to do is discussion about an item (or a brand) you like, let your readers know how you use it, and illuminate them how they can profit from it too. Presently, the amount you procure depends, once more, on a few factors: the niche you're in, how frequently you compose sponsored posts, who pays you, and so forth. Installments range from two or three hundred bucks to a few thousand bucks for every post, except at times likewise a huge number of dollars in the event that your site has a great deal of traffic.

Presently, something essential to recollect while composing a sponsored post is that you ought to by and large expound on items and organizations that you like, trust, and really have tested. These ought to be brands and organizations that you really feel better about, that you put stock in, and don't have an issue promoting. Like that, it'll be a lot simpler to acquire trust with your readers since, supposing that they don't believe you're genuine, it'll hurt your site's growth.

On the off chance that you're still sitting in the fence, here are a few upsides and downsides of supported blog entries.

A Prologue To Sponsored Blog Posts

Despite the fact that "sponsored blog post" could mean a wide range of things, we're discussing a post an organization pays you to write on your own blog. They do this as a method for introducing themselves or their item to your audience. As a blogger, you have a 'platform' that can be entirely important to those with an engaging product who need to edge a spotlight on your readers.

These sorts of posts can be product, reviews, proposals, or an article about the organization with links to authentic landing pages. Regularly, you'll compose the content (or possibly commission it from a writer), yet it is sometimes given to you. One way or the other, they are intended to be enlightening and helpful to your audience rather than an Ad.

For instance, the coffee analyst site frequently composes reviews of new items on their blog: Since they have dedicated followers of coffee lovers who trust the website, the blog posts are significant to organizations searching for a method for advancing new items in this niche. In that capacity, any highlighted reviews let the news out and assist with boost sales. For this reason sponsored blog post are an incredible way for you to make extra pay. They are one of the main ways of adapting your blog, and there are great deals for organizations hoping to contain this method as a component of their promoting efforts. In any case, you should be mindful so as to comply to Federal Trade Commission (FTC) guidelines, which expect you to reveal in your post who you are working with. In the post above, coffee detective puts this note at the end of the audit: It's likewise important to be particular with your sponsors. Each brand you feature ought to match with your qualities and appeal to your readers. Something too misguided may seem to be malicious and switch off your crowd.

How to get sponsored blog posts (6 key tips)

In spite of the fact that supported posts is a good method for expanding your income, getting them is different. The following are six vital ways to land sponsored posts for your blog!

1. Set up a sponsor page and media unit on your site

Perhaps the first (and simplest) ways of getting sponsored blog post is to place a page on your site welcoming pitches. This is an incredible, direct approach to telling individuals you're free to get sponsored posts. For instance, you can see this method in real life on TayTalksMoney:

Furthermore, you can offer a media kit to assist those wishing to bargain with you. As a matter of fact, a few organizations will request to see your media kit as a matter of fact before choosing to work with you. Your media pack can include the following:

- Name

- Contact data

- Site name and URL

- Social stats - the informal communities you use and your number of devotees, and so on.

- Month to month site visits on your site - you can involve Google analytics for this

- A little about your audience

- Some information about what you bring to the table

An expert media kit shows that you're significant and searching for supports. Consider it a resume for you, your platform, and your blog. Accordingly, you'll need to make it convincing.

2. Make top-quality content that draws in sponsors

Quality content is the core of your blog. With it, you can draw in readers and committed follower to your site. In addition, with enough quality substance, you can develop your audience and your foundation - and brands might start wanting to deal with you.

In general, your content ought to constantly look forward to offering great benefit to your readers. Nonetheless, most importantly before you can draw in sponsors, you might have to lay out a reliable name in your specialty. Whenever you've constructed a stage and turned into a pro in your field, you can then start taking on sponsored blog posts. Thusly, this tip addresses a 'slow-burner,' and takes times to implement.

3. Find brands you want to work with and pitch sponsored post ideas to them

Whenever you've set up a support page and a media pack, and your blog is loaded up with top notch content, you might need to start testing out a few sponsored post ideas on brands in your specialty. Many organizations will have links on their sites where you can get in touch with them and propose your thought. An effective method for moving toward this is to begin with product you as of now use and like. For instance, if that there's one you truly appreciate utilizing, and consider it would be a decent fit for your audience, consider contacting the organization with a proposition. Some have even made progress by referencing helpful brands via the social media. Assuming the objective organization sees your notices, they might reach you straightforwardly to check whether you're keen on cooperating. Thinking outside the box with regards to getting organizations to notice you is vital.

4. Take a gander at your opposition and see who's sponsoring them

Another effective method for finding sponsors is to examine your oppositions and see who is being placed on their blog. Chances are, in the event that they are keen on working with them, they might be keen on having a few posts put with you too.

This is particularly successful if write in a small niche. There may not be an excessive number of individuals working in your field and sponsorship open doors might be limited. If so, organizations hoping to broaden their compass might be glad to hear from you and happily seize the opportunity of a sponsored post on your blog.

5. Pitch sponsorships to the brands you find in Google AdSense

Assuming that you use Google AdSense, you'll see what kinds of brands are drawn to your site before long. This is a powerful method for tracking down additional brands to pitch your sponsored post service to.

For instance, think about the following adverts:

if you're in the right business and niche and your size and target readers is adequate - Mazda might be an organization worth connecting with. While pitching to these brands, try to enlighten them concerning you, your site, your readership, and how you are willingly to work with them. Your media kit will definitely become possibly the most important factor here. This will give the organization the information they need to make an option and smoothes the relationship up-front.

6. Maintain relationships with sponsors to receive more promotions over time

At last, one of the most outstanding ways of building a strong and lasting income with your blog is to work with similar brands more than once. Assuming that you keep up with the connections you develop, organizations are bound to recruit you again for future sponsored blog post.

Accordingly, this is a motivator to go about your absolute best responsibilities. The more grounded your sponsored posts are, the more likely they are to succeed for both you and the Sponsors. To keep up with your connections, be obliging and professional, be open with your correspondence, and have an positive approach to their project. It as well assists with doing precisely exact thing you say you will do.

Advantages And Disadvantages Of Supported Blog Entries:
Advantages: You'll bring in more cash

Regularly, when you start a blog, one of your fundamental objectives is to bring in cash. Regardless of whether it's not the primary explanation you began it, the way that you're bringing in cash from your blog is an or more. Supported posts are a simple method for adapting your blog.

Disadvantages: It's takes a lot to manage

Assuming that you're the solitary author and proprietor of your blog, adding sponsored posts presumably won't add a lot of administrative work to your plate. In the event that you've proactively got a couple of individuals who compose for you, adding sponsored posts could make more work for you. There's the editing, style guide, and back linking you must check. You must check for replica content, plagiarized content, from there, the sky is the limit. It can appear to be overpowering on the off chance that you're not accustomed to it, regardless of whether they are paying you for it.

Advantage: It's a sign your blog is developing

Being approached by a brand or organization to publicize to your readers implies you've ever figured things out rightly with your blog. You've turned into trusted voice and master pioneer on that very niche, and the brand needs to collaborate with you! That can be a great vibe.

Disadvantage: You've already got a ton of other advert on your blog

If sponsored posts become your seventh or eighth approach to monetizing your blog, you should hold off on tolerating them. Every single one of these monetization channels can present to you a decent pay. In any case, assuming your site is loaded up with them, your readers will be switched off.

There's nothing more regrettable than exploring to a site with affiliate links, adverts in the sidebar, inline adverts all through each post, and in the footers. It occupies from your message and diminishes the trust your readers have in you. Since it has become so obvious what a sponsored post is and why you ought to consider them for your blog, we should find how you can manage these sponsored posts. You'll have a tad of schoolwork to do before you can open your blog to sponsored posts.

There's nothing more horrible than exploring a site with, adverts in the sidebar, affiliate links and also inline advert generally through each post, and in the footers. It occupies from your message and decreases the trust your readers have in you. Since it has become so blatantly clear what an sponsored post is and why you should consider them for your blog, we ought to find how you need to make arrangements for sponsored posts. You'll have a dab of homework to do before you can open your blog to sponsored posts.

What You Need Before You Get Started (Checklist)

sponsors wnts to work with a blog that has a long record of posting, a solid and drew in engaged audience, and is pertinent to their product or services. While it would be good to begin getting sponsors with a new blog, the odds are, you will not.

Thus, in the event that you might want to draw in sponsors to your blog, the following are a couple of things they search for:

• **Sound Traffic Rates:** You ought to have a constant flow of traffic to your blog that trends up each month. You can make sense of the internet marketing systems you use to accomplish this and what your marketing objectives are for the year. Assuming that your traffic is low, look at my guide on the most proficient method to get more traffic to your blog.

• **Social Media Following:** Moreover, your blog's virtual entertainment records ought to have a sound following of engaged individuals. As the blog proprietor, you ought to be taking part in the discussions individuals have with your blog and brand, encouraging individuals to keep talk.

• **High Domain Authority (DA):** While DA isn't the be-all measurement for sponsors, it shows how very much regarded your blog is, demonstrates you have a ton of top notch backlinks, and predicts that their sponsored posts have a decent shot at showing up high up on search engines report page. Blogs with DA scores of 30+ will have a superior chance of securing sponsored posts.

- **Clean and Simple Site Structure:** A simple to-use webpage structure is an indication of an efficient blog that is well managed. It likewise makes it more straightforward for search engines to catalog, meaning it has a superior chance to rank high with them.

How Much Should You Charge For Sponsored Posts?

To put it plainly, it depends. The going rates for sponsored blog entries differ fiercely, contingent upon the market or niche you're in, rivalry, current economic situations, brand advertising budgets, your blog webpage details, and so on.

besides, how might you figure out what you ought to charge for supported blog entries?

- You could begin by taking a gander at your opponent to check whether they're tolerating sponsored posts. What do they charge for them? Do they publish their charges on the web? Taking a gander at what different bloggers charge for supported posts can assist you with deciding your price.

- You could likewise request that your organization check whether anybody will share their rates. You might know different bloggers who concede sponsored posts, yet you've never stopped to get some information about it. Take a look at marketing organization sites to check whether they offer sponsored posts as a component of their administrations. Provided that this is true, consider messaging them to check whether they'd chat with you about contributing to a blog, and you can ask them for a cost range for the service.

As we mentioned, your supported post rates will depend upon various elements encompassing your site, yet additionally the actual post. Whenever you've sorted out a general rate, you might need to consider having 2 rates:

1. One for posts you compose in light of a sponsors resources.

2. One for posts the sponsor composes in based of your rules.

On the off chance that you're composing and researching the post, the charge ought to be somewhat more than if your sponsor is composing it. You'll need to be compensated for both your time and viewers.

Setting your sponsored post rates is somewhat of a fine art, thus, you'll simply need to make a plunge and pick a number at one point. Ensure it's a number you're OK with, then, change it in light of the reaction from sponsors and conversations you might have with them.

Factors to Consider Before Accepting Sponsored Posts

At the point when a sponsor applies to compose for your blog, you ought to think about a couple of elements as a component of your interaction. These elements may adversely affect your blog if you don't watch out, which then, at that point, could prompt less sponsors later on and lower expenses they're willing to pay.

Additionally, you'll harm your standing with your audience since they'll not be keen on the substance. They'll believe you're simply distributing it for the cash, not on the grounds that you thought it was important data. Keep in mind, all the substance you distribute on your blog ought to enhance the live of your audience.

What you need to look out for in a sponsor: A Sponsor's Fit for Your Blog and Audience

Sponsors are ideal for your blog assuming they're from an organization, business, or brand that is connected with your blog's niche, subject, or market. For instance, in the event that you possessed a pet blog, you won't distribute a supported post from a printing company. Pick a pet company all things being equal!

if you're considering distributing sponsored content that doesn't fit your site under any condition, don't. The primary thing to recollect about supported posts is that they're most captivating when the sponsor as of now focuses on your blog's main fans with their products, and the post examines points that line up with your brand. At the point when getting along admirably, any notice of the sponsors brand feels like a characteristic fit rather than an explicit ad. Readers ought to leave sponsored post feeling like they've discovered some new information. This makes your blog more tenable, significant, and dependable. Some blog specialists will tell you to "never" acknowledge sponsored posts since it'll "ruin" your blog. In any case, that is false. However as long you incorporate the sponsored substance honestly and guarantee it of usefulness to your readers, it shouldn't make any difference.

A Sponsor's Google Ranking

All links on your blog are subject to indexing by Google and influence how it positions your pages and domain. Google punishes paid links, so to keep away from this, add the "no follow" attribute to all links in your sponsored posts. This advises Google to overlook these connections in rankings and spare your domain and pages any punishments.

There are two methods for doing this on a WordPress blog: either manually by adding the HTML code to each link or with a WordPress plugin that does it for you if you're actually utilizing the classic editor.

To add the no follow HTML code manually:

- Edit the supported post in your WordPress dashboard.

- Open the Code Editor if utilizing Gutenberg or Text Editor tool if utilizing the old editor.

- Inside the HTML code for every hyperlink (<a>) add rel="nofollow" after the URL. For instance, change <a href="http://blogtyrant.com">Blog Tyrant</a> to <a href="http://blogtyrant.com" rel="nofollow">Blog Tyrant</a>.

You can likewise utilize a WordPress plugin to roll out these changes, like All in One SEO. All in One SEO makes it really simple to control inside and outside links in your content.

The main issue with adding the nofollow characteristic to these links is that your readers are incompletely paying for this extra SEO Exposure and won't want that it be added to their links. You should be straightforward with this to your sponsors so they can conclude whether that's completely fine.

Most sponsored post organizations comprehend in light of the fact that their fundamental reason for supporting content is for brand awareness in a more extensive audience. They'll take any extra Web optimization they get from it, however it's not their essential concentration. Be careful about the ones who are resolute about not adding the nofollow trait to their sponsored posts.

The Amount of Sponsored Posts You Publish

At the point when you distribute sponsored posts, you're telling your readers you trust in the item or service so much, and you needed to tell them about it. They like your blog for you, not the sponsors, but they comprehend the fact that you have to bring in a income with your blog. What's a decent schedule for distributing sponsored posts? Indeed, it depends on you and your audience propensities, bu you could:

- Distribute them one time per month.

- Distribute one after each 5 of your own posts.

- Spread the supported posts in every one of your blog's category. For instance, in the event that you run a food blog, you could distribute one under "recipes", one under "reviews", and one more under "shopping."

- Only acknowledge supported posts that fit a single category, related to "reviws."

It'll be more straightforward to distribute the supported posts on your blog whenever you've been around for some time. You might have to test what turns out best for your blog, however don't be bashful about altering the manner in which you distribute them in the event that you find out it's not working for your blog or audience. Anything that you schedule, ensure you don't irritate your readers. You would rather not break that obligation of trust you've developed with them. Be that as it may, you can definitely relax, they'll inform you as to whether you distribute too much. You'll see your site details drop and they'll quit drawing in with you. Stick to distributing quality, authentic content and your audience will hold on to returning to your blog.

We've covered every one of the contemplations and consideration to look out for with sponsored posts. This is the way you can get everything rolling with supported posts for your blog.

How to Get Started With Sponsored Posts (Step-by-Step)

Here are 6 easy steps you can use to get started with sponsored posts on your blog.

Stage 1: Accumulate Your Site Data

You'll require every one of the details concerning your blog that a sponsor could get to ask about, including:

- **Site stats:** visitor numbers, bounce rate rate, CTR (click through rate), area authority, and web search tool traffic details for high-performing pages.

- **social media stats:** Number of followers on your picked channels, number of remarks on blog entries, and so on.

- **Email list:** Number of individuals on your rundown, the number of you add each week/month, the development of your email list, and commitment rates (open and click rates).

Remember to have two or three lines making sense of your blog's aim or objective, who your audience is, and the way that you desire to help them.

Stage 2: Settle on Your sponsored Post fees

Make a list of the kind of sponsored posts you'll acknowledge and what you charge for them. Make certain to incorporate data like length, the quantity of backlinks, subjects to expound on, and stay away from. You can list this data on a page on your blog, or as a downloadable PDF.

Additionally, make a point to set your installment technique and installment strategy so that organizations know how and when to pay you. Many supporters won't have any desire to pay until the post is distributed, so you could want installment inside 10-15 work days after posting. Make sure to likewise incorporate a strategy about what occurs on the off chance that you are not paid on time and assuming you'll eliminate the post assuming that occurs.

Stage 3: Make a Supported Posts Page

A supported posts page is where brands will apply to your supported post program.

Create a landing page that frames the data you accumulated in the first step, for example, main interest group numbers, details on site visits, web crawler traffic numbers, virtual entertainment supporters, media appearances, and talking commitment.

You can simply make a presentation page with SeedProd. SeedProd offers an intuitive manufacturer and more than 100 landing page templates so you can get rapidly.

A few sites acknowledge sponsored post request through email, however you can likewise add a structure that will deal with the solicitations for you. Fortunately, SeedProd coordinates with WPForms, so you can make a blog entry accommodation structure that will send them naturally to you.

WP Structures likewise has installment additional items that will coordinate PayPal, Stripe, or another installment processor. This allows you to gather the supported post expenses immediately from the structure. Utilize these directions to set up a paid blog entry accommodation structure with WPForms.

On your post landing page, make certain to outline the sponsorship levels so organizations realize the amount it'll cost them, what they receive consequently, and any arrangements you could have for the content. Furthermore, make certain to add all the data a sponsor ought to be familiar with the stuff to compose for your blog, for example, spelling rules, style guidelines, brand notices, and how they ought to present a request. This would be the spot to publish your sponsorship charges also, if you need to promote them. You can constantly connect them through a downloadable PDF file if you don't need then showing on the page directly.

When you've made the landing page, add it to your navigation menu anywhere, as in a sub-menu of your menu. landing a greeting page like this will make it simpler for brands to reach out for you about sponsored posts.

Step 4: Document Your Process & Publish Your Disclosure Policy

Create a document with your sponsored post program data, including your expenses, installments, whether you'll utilize the nofollow attribute, how long you'll keep the post on your site (most are kept live for one year), and so on. Store this data in a protected place so you can refer to it depending on the situation.

You'll likewise have to make and publish a disclosure strategy for your site. The American Federal Trade Commission (FTC) has severe rules encompassing paying for online posts and promoting, and solid fines for brands and online properties (like your blog) that abuse them. Other worldwide regulations might apply to your blog, as well, so be certain you know all about them and how to comply. They're normally applicable in view of where you reside and where your site is based, so cousult the data for your location as applicable.

We are not lawyers, and the above ought not be taken or understood as legal advice. Consult a nearby legal practitioner for additional subtleties.

In general, your blog or site, by and large, must:

• Ensure all your content is liberated from misdirecting claims or lies. For instance, saying an item can fix a disease when the brand has not demonstrated it can do as such.

• Obviously unveil that a post is sponsored in each post, even via social media. This tells crowds some or the content was all paid for.

• Include a disclosure report for your site that you acknowledge paid posts. This is notwithstanding the individual disclosure you make on each sponsored post.

• Make the statement legible on all gadgets, including cell phones.

Step 6: Attract Sponsors

You're almost prepared to begin distributing sponsored posts on your blog, right? However, imagine a scenario where, sooner or later, you're attracting anybody to sponsor content on your blog. Now is the right time to begin promoting your accessibility to sponsors. Very much like you advertised your blog to the world to find readers, you should be proactive in tracking down organizations to sponsor content on your blog. There are multiple ways you can do that;

• You can search out brands you like and pitch them. Make sure to key in on how you can help the brand and not how they'll help you.

- Look for nearby businesses that might fit your blog's audience. These organizations might struggle to advertise beyond their region, so your blog could assist them with expanding recongnition to a more extensive audience.

- Foster associations with marketing and PR agencies. They frequently search for spots to put content for their clients and usually need a large number of bloggers to address their clients' requests.

- Investigate sponsored post sites or commercial centers like Cooperative, SeedingUp, Izea, PayPerPost, Markerly, TapInfluence, , and GetReviewed. These services connects brands with bloggers hoping to monetize their sites and can be a decent choice for you since they accomplish the duty of tracking down the sponsors. You can focus on composing great content and less on marketing.

Additionally, remember to compose a periodic post explaining that you acknowledge sponsors as well. You might have expected sponsors in your readership who don't realize they could sponsor content on the blog. Thus, let them know occasionally.

Finally in this manual for sponsored content: how to compose sponsored content. A few sponsor will give the content to distribute on your blog, while others will believe you should compose it for them. Assuming that is the situation, we have got you covered on certain tips on the best way to do that.

Three Tips for Writing Sponsored Posts

- Bear in mind that the sponsored content should fulfill your blog's guidelines. It ought to be pleasant to read and contain a lot of important information for the audience. sponsored content ought to attract and please your readers, so they keep coming back.

- Keep up with your voice and brand in the sponsored content. The sponsors item, service, or brand ought to be optional to the content primary focus, except if it's an prduct review or something to that effect. Your readers will back out on the if the post feels like it's simply an ad for the sponsor.

- Distribute an assortment of blog entry types for supports. Make one a bullet point article, one a contextual investigation, one a plain post, one with loads of pictures, one that is only a video post, and so on. Keep it in accordance with the remainder of your blog entry types, however make it fascinating to perusers.

writing supported content is an extraordinary method for monetizing your blog, yet once in a while, offsetting sponsored necessities with your credible voice can be a test. Considering that, we've concocted 10 prescribed procedures for composing supported content that will assist you with remaining consistent with your blog while building your business.

Make it personal

Readers follow your blog since they like your voice and your viewpoint (regardless of whether they generally concur with it). Particularly with regards to brand supported blog, first-person experiences and stories are vital. Except if it's proper, share your story, not another person's.

Keep your post between 200-600 words

While making content for a brand, likewise with most of blog content, posts ought to be sufficiently long to offer significant knowledge and data, yet short to the point of keeping the attention of your readers. Frequently, the end of a sponsored post has a significant source of inspiration or information, so managing length is a significant element to keeping both the brand blissful and your audience locked in.

Use rich media like images and video

Blog posts that include pictures, designs, photos or video are considerably more captivating than posts that don't. At the point when posts are supplemented with rich pictures or sight and sound, readers stay longer on your site and are bound to share your post on other social media handles. Multimedia content is gold to a brand and will make you stand amongst different publishers. New photography and video applications make it really simple to make fun content. Discover some that you like (our favs include DipTic, CameraSharp, GroupShot, Promote, Klip and Viddy) and get everything rolling!

Stay bona fide to your voice

Brands come to you because you understand how to really draw in your listeners, and you've constructed a blog and brand with your unique voice so don't forfeit it! By remaining consistent with your style and character, a sponsored post won't stand out in contrast to everything else and your readers will realize you're being genuine, which prompts the following point.

If you dislike a product you've been paid to review, get in touch with your brand or agency contact

If you realize you dislike a brand or product don't accept the program. Notwithstanding, if you're obliged to post as a section of an on-going project and you find out that you also dislike disdain an item as well as subject, reach out to the program director, tell the truth. There's most likely an answer that will ensure the integrity of both the blogger and brand, and they will be pleased about you attempting to track down an solutions. This present circumstance is a problem turned opportunity to fabricate trust and regard with clients.

Use SEO keywords and expressions

Assuming a brand gives you a FAQ or extra product information, they might include Search engine optimization (SEO) keywords and expressions that they are driving for a specific campaign. Your blog will see more traffic when those keyswords or expressions are searched (and for campaign inside your niche, you could get new devoted readers), and subsequently the brand will get more traffic through your sponsored post.

Be clear about payment

If you're being paid for a post, ensure your readers are somewhat familiar with it. In addition to the fact that it is essential to keep up with the trust of your audience, however you're expected by the FTC disclosure Guidelines to uncover when you're getting financial compensation for a review, mention or sponsored post.

Be accountable

Have a sense of ownership with understanding what is generally expected of you (when a post is expected, the amount you will get paid, the number of words if pertinent, what should be included, etc). If any of the terms are confusing or fluffy, connect with your agency or brand contact and find out. We all have disturbance in our schedules however don't allow an individual hiccup to hold you back from being accountable. On the off chance that you can't make your time limit, let your contact know so they are not left looking for your post a few days after its due date. Be as profession and proficient with your brand contacts as you would like them to go along with you.

Exceed expectations

At the point when a brand is paying you, they are your customer. Charming and captivating your clients make them need to work with you once more and will motivate them to praise you. Very much like with items, it is more affordable to get existing clients to return than it is to join new clients. While it's unquestionably not needed, exceeding everyone's expectations or adding an exceptional component to your supported post goes quite far!

Tell a decent story

A good story is a flair. Certain individuals are naturals and a few of us need a touch of coaching to capture the hearts of our readers with our stories, as a matter of fact. Affiliate marketing is based on the idea of banding together brands with bloggers who offer related content and having those brands sponsor those stories. Brands find bloggers strong in view of the stories and the credible content they make. Components that cause a good story include keeping it honest and sincere, allowing the readers to feel like they are in the background, and dealing with individuals in your accounts like they are characters. Great stories have a spine subject with a beginning, central and end. Put yourself out there a little and you'll be shocked at how profoundly you'll contact more audience.

Be proactive

The most effective way to find sponsors for your blog is by being proactive. You could make an expert media kit, find brands you desire to work with, and pitch a sponsored post to them. In a twinkle, you'll have organizations paying you to write on your own blog.

CHAPTER FOUR
AFFILIATE MARKETING

What is affiliate marketing?

Affiliate marketing is where you advance an organization's item or administration as a trade-off for a commission on the deals you create. Commissions are ordinarily a level of the deal value, however can sometimes be a fixed sum.

Affiliate marketing is most certainly one of the most incredible ways of bringing in cash online. Certainly, individuals live off a affiliate connections since they procure four, five, and six figures every month! You can check Michelle Schroeder-Gardner's seminar on the best way to do this appropriately. All things considered, she makes $100,000 every month from Affiliate marketing. Obviously, likewise with different sorts of paid web-based work and advertising, the amount you acquire from Affiliate marketing relies upon the specialty you're working in. A few organizations will pay even up to $100 per transformation.

Specialties like monetary preparation and internet banking, as well as financial planning, credit cards, and Bitcoin, offer very great cash for Affiliate links. There are additionally other member specialties that are developing increasingly more with time, including health, wellness, dieting, leisure activity specialties like travel and photography, and, obviously, innovation. Web facilitating is one of the most rewarding subsidiary showcasing specialties, where organizations offer up to $500 per deal to members for each new client they allude to them. If you have any desire to begin with Affiliate marketing, you should pursue partner programs on the sites of the organizations you need to work with. Each organization will have its own tips on how you can do this and its own arrangements of standards you really want to persuade to be qualified for their partner programs. On the off chance that you're new to Affiliate marketing and need to figure out how everything for the most part functions, then I propose you make a gander at this stride by-step YouTube video for member showcasing fledglings, it's truly helpful.

Imagine all you expectations to bring in cash online was just embedded in having a site. You don't need to make your own items or deal a help. Sounds great? Welcome to Affiliate marketing. As per Measurements, business spending on subsidiary showc Affiliate marketing asing will hit $9.2 billion in the U.S by 2023.

How to get started with affiliate marketing

Follow these seven basic advances.

1. Decide on a forum
2. Choose your specialty
3. Find affiliate projects to join
4. Create incredible substance
5. Drive traffic to your member site
6. Get snaps on your member joins
7. Convert snaps to deals

1. Decide on a forum

Hypothetically, you can do affiliate marketing on any forum. Indeed, even Instagram works. In any case, it's a lot simpler to fabricate a crowd of people and increment your subsidiary deals through one of two channels: a blog or YouTube channel.

Beginning a blog today is generally simple and modest. There are a lot of instructional exercises online that show you how to begin. The greatest aspect? It'll probably just expense you a couple of dollars each month. When your site is up, streamline it for web search tools with the goal that you have a superior possibility positioning. From that point, you're allowed to add affiliate links in your substance. (There is a craftsmanship to doing this, which we'll cover later in this aide.)

The other stage is YouTube. Making and transferring content to YouTube is free, which makes it ideal for some individuals. Upgrade your recordings for Website design enhancement, and incorporate associate connections in your portrayal. Note that you'll have to uncover the way that you're including associate connections. The Government Exchange Commissions (FTC) expects you to be straightforward while getting pay from a support.

In the event that you're utilizing a blog, make an independent page, or remember it for the footer of your site like this: Assuming you're doing it on YouTube, remember it for your depiction. Presently, you'll probably get a larger number of snaps from a blog than a YouTube video. Thus, the vast majority of the models proceeding will be for a blog.

2. **Choose your specialty**

Can we just look at things objectively for a moment on the off chance that you're beginning a blog today; you're confronting a lot of rivalry. Measurements gauges that the quantity of bloggers in the U.S will reach 41.7 million by 2023. To have the best potential for success of progress, niche down.

Pick a topic that spotlights on a particular category. For instance, the subject of "food" is a tremendous category. As opposed to handling that, take a crack at something more unambiguous, such as grilling food. Keeping your topic tight can assist you with building a more engaged crowd and possibly assist you with positioning higher in web crawlers. That is the thing I did when I assembled my most memorable site. Rather than discussing "dance" or "hip hop," I chose to restrict myself to simply break dancing. In spite of knowing nothing about Website design enhancement in those days, I figured out how to rank for a couple of key terms and produce ~3,000 natural visits each month. Later on, as you cover the greater part of this classification and construct traffic to these pages, you can venture into different areas.

Presently, assuming you will be the main content creator, pick something you're keen on. Many affiliate sites pass on because of an absence of consistency. So in any event, on the off chance that you're enthusiastic about a point, you'll find it a lot simpler to press on whenever hardship rears it. Simply sit back and relax if you're not a specialist in the field. As Gary Vaynerchuk puts it, "document, don't create." Reporting what you've realized can make extraordinary substance and draw in individuals who are keen on following your advancement. On the off chance that you're reevaluating the substance, it's smarter to work with prepared specialists in the specialty. experts can assist you with making top caliber, trustworthy work, which can prompt more traffic, draw in guests, and more affiliate sales.

3.   **Find subsidiary projects to join**

There are three kinds of subsidiary projects to look over.

A. High-paying, low-volume affiliate programs

These are member programs for specialty items with high payouts. For instance, ConvertKit's member program pays nearly $700 each month assuming that you send only 80 clients their way. Be that as it may, as they sell CRM programming for entrepreneurs, there's a restricted pool of purchasers. Moreover there may be more contest for programs with high commissions. Since you're presumably beginning, it'll be very difficult to bring in a significant measure of cash going up against gifted advertisers with abundant resources.

B. Low-paying, high-volume *affiliate* programs

These are affiliate programs for items with low payouts yet mass allure. For instance, take PS4 games. Bunches of individuals play PS4, yet the normal expense of a game is just around $50, and member commissions are as a rule in the single digits. This implies you'll acquire $2-3 for each deal given that you're fortunate. The saving grace of these kinds of projects is that they normally offer lots of items to sell. Take Amazon's member program, for instance. You can acquire up to 10% commissions on nearly anything Amazon sells.

The other beneficial thing is that you frequently get commissions on the whole worth of the buy as opposed to only the item you suggested. To make these kinds of subsidiary projects pay, you'll require tons of traffic.

C. Lucrative, high-volume member programs

These are member programs for items with mass allure, which additionally pay high commissions. One model is credit cards. Everybody needs a credit card, and a great many people stay with the organization for quite a long time (in some cases even many years!)

The drawback of these kinds of items is that they draw in partner advertisers with plenty of mastery and deep pockets. Some additionally use vicious strategies that you can't contend with. Furthermore, since this is an instructional exercise for begineers, I will not go any more profound into this. Simply know that these projects exist.

How To Decide Which Affiliate Programs To Join

This relies upon your specialty and level of expertise. If you're focusing on buyers, you'll probably go with the second model of low commissions and higher sales volume. On the off chance that you're pursuing an audience, you'll probably go for the first model: lucrative and low volume. The most famous projects here are for programming and web facilitating related items.

The most ideal way to find these offshoot programs is with a Google search. On the other hand, enter a contending affiliate site into Ahrefs' Site Traveler and go to the Connected domains report. For instance, I realize that Pat Flynn advances various programming items on his site, Brilliant Automated revenue. Eyeballing the Connected domains report shows that Pat connects to a Weber pretty frequently.

It just takes a fast Google search to find an application structure for this program. Notwithstanding, on the off chance that there is an item you'd truly prefer to advance without a public subsidiary program, contact the organization and inquire as to whether they might want to fabricate a partner relationship with you.

4.   Create amazing content

In the event that you need your partner site to succeed, you really want to make great substance where your subsidiary connections fit normally. Here is a model. Tim Ferriss talked with 100+ celebrities and posed them this query: What acquisition of $100 or less has most decidedly affected your life over the most recent a half year (or in current memory)? He distributed the responses in a blog entry and included affiliate links to the items referenced:

According to the remarks, his fans adored it. This is the very thing you need to copy while making content for your affiliate site. Don't simply indiscriminately arrange items from Amazon's hits. Go above and beyond to ensure your substance tackles the visitors concern. How? Assuming you're doing audits, really buy the item and test it. This is the very thing that the Wirecutter did, which makes sense of their success. In the event that you don't have the means to purchase each and every item, you can constantly begin with what you have at home. For instance, in the event that you had a tech blog, you could make surveys on the devices you own.

5.   Drive traffic to your affiliate site

You've made incredible substance. The following stage is to get more individuals to understand it, so they will tap on your partner joins. The following are three traffic methodologies to consider:

A. Paid traffic

This is where you pay for traffic to your site. You can do this utilizing PPC promotions. The upside of paid traffic is that the second you begin paying, you get traffic. Nonetheless, there are a few drawbacks.

To start with, running advertisements will dive into your benefits. It's very typical for sponsors to lose cash before they make it… assuming they at any point do. You should be reasonable about what amount of time it requires to improve a paid traffic crusade.

Furthermore, when you quit paying for promotions, your traffic will stop. Promotions, by and large, are an extraordinary traffic procedure in the event that you're essential for a lucrative partner program and can make the numbers work. In any case, in the event that you're totally new to paid marketing and have no marketing arrangement (or are working with lower commission programs like Amazon Partners), then it probably won't be a particularly good thought

B. Search engine optimization (SEO)

SEO is the act of upgrading pages to rank high in web search tools like Google. However, as long you can rank high in the web crawlers for your objective watchwords, you'll get reliable and latent traffic.

On the most fundamental level, Website optimization is about:

- Understanding what your objective clients are looking for;

- Making content around those themes (blog entries, item pages, and so on.);

- Dealing with the "technical" stuff to push these pages higher in the web crawlers (which incorporates external link establishment).

C. produce an email list

Email records permit you to speak with your readers at any time. Use them to enlighten fans concerning new content and keep them returning to your site for more. This prompts more member snaps and deals. You could send subsidiary email advancements to your list candidly:

To fabricate an email show, you really want to convince the reader on your site to join. That implies offering something significant.

6. Get snaps on your affiliate links

Since you have an astounding piece of content doesn't mean individuals will tap on your affiliate links. There are a couple of things you really want to consider.

A. Link placement

In the event that all your subsidiary connections are at the lower part of the page where individuals seldomly scroll, clicks will be rare. Then again, make each and every other word a connection in your presentation, and your content will look cruel. You need to offset interface position with the other factors underneath.

B. Context

Suppose you were composing an article on the best kitchen blades for under $50. Your introduction presumably should seem to be something like this: Today, I'm looking into three changed culinary specialist blades you can purchase on Amazon for under $50. These are, item name 1, item name 2, and item name 3..

C. Callouts

Utilizing callouts like buttons, tables, and boxes can assist with standing out for your readers and make the post more appropriate. For instance, the Wirecutter utilizes eye-getting boxes with product links whenever they share a top pick. PC Macintosh adopts an alternate strategy and utilizes a parallel table with buttons:

7. Convert snaps to deals

In affiliate marketing, two transformations need to happen for you to bring in cash. The main change is the snap to the item page. You're 100 percent in charge of this action. Utilize the strategies above to work on your possibilities getting that click.

The second change is the guest buying the product. On account of affiliate marketing, the dealer controls the checkout, and their transformation rates are beyond your control. Try to play the game for your potential benefit and search for traders with programs that convert well. The following are a couple of ways of tracking down them:

A. Public income reports

In the event that individuals are bringing in good cash from an affiliate program, almost certainly, the item changes over well. How can you say whether individuals are bringing in cash? Take a gander at public income reports where bloggers freely uncover how much cash they're making from their affiliate deals. You can track down these reports on Google.

For instance, in the event that you look for "income report amazon affiliate", you'll see a couple of blog entries showing how bloggers have brought in cash as Amazon Members, Seems as though one blogger made $7,300 in a solitary month from Amazon commissions. In the event that you're in a similar space, you can likewise investigate where her other subsidiary pay comes from, and possibly promote similar products.

B. Get clarification on pressing issues

On the off chance that there isn't a lot of information about an affiliate program you need to join, join and seek clarification on some pressing issues. For instance, you should figure out what their typical conversion rates are, or a rough estimate of their top workers' month to month commissions. This can assist you with sorting out whether or not the affiliate program merits advancing.

C. Use your instinct

Now and then, it's ideal to go with your instinct. In the event that the program or item you're looking at feels "off," or on the other hand assuming you would never prescribe the item to a companion or relative, then don't promote it.

How Does Affiliate Marketing Work?

Since subsidiary showcasing works by spreading the obligations of item promoting and creation across parties, it use the capacities of various people for a more powerful advertising procedure while furnishing patrons with a portion of the benefit. To make this work, three unique parties should be involved:

1. Seller and item creators.

2. The affiliate or promoter.

3. The consumer.

We should dive into the perplexing relationship these three parties offer to guarantee affilaite marketing is a success:

1. Seller and item creators

The dealer, whether an independent business person or enormous enterprise, is a seller, shipper, vendor, merchant, item maker or retailer with an item to showcase. The product can be an physical product , similar to family products, or a service, similar to makeup tutorials, also known as the brand, the dealer needn't bother with to be effectively engaged with the promoting, however they may likewise be the promoter and benefit from the income sharing related with affiliate marketing. For instance, the seller could be an online business dealer that began an affiliate business and needs to contact other clients by paying affiliates links to promote their items. Or on the other hand the seller could be a SAAS company that use offshoots to assist with selling their marketing programming.

2. The affiliate or publisher

Otherwise called a publisher, the affiliate can be either an individual or an organization that showcases the sellers item in an attractive manner to expected customers. All in all, the affiliates elevate the product to convince shoppers that it is significant or valuable to them and persuade them to buy the product. In the event that the customer winds up purchasing the item, the affiliate gets a piece of the income made.

Partners frequently have a quite certain crowd to whom they market, by and large sticking to that crowd's advantages. This makes a characterized specialty or individual brand that assists the affiliate with drawing in customers who will be probably going to follow up on the advertising.

3. The consumer

Obviously, for the subsidiary framework to work, there should be sales and the consumer or client is the person who gets them going. The affiliate will showcase the product to shoppers through the fundamental channel(s), whether it be virtual entertainment, a blog or a YouTube video, and in the event that the customer considers the item as significant or valuable to them, they can follow the affiliate links and checkout on the sellers site. On the off chance that the client buys the thing, the affiliate gets a piece of the income made. Notwithstanding, remember that the client should know that you, the member, are getting a commission off the item.

As per the Government Exchange Commission, an affiliate marketer advertiser should obviously and prominently unveil their relationship to the retailer, hence permitting the buyer to conclude how much weight to give your endorsement.

Types of Affiliate Marketing

It's uncertain whether an affiliate marketer has really utilized the item they're promoting or on the other hand on the off chance that they're basically in it for the cash — at times it may not make any difference to the client without a doubt. In any case, different times, for example, with diet services or skincare product, the client may not believe a subsidiary except if they know that he/she has tried and endorsed the actual product.

In 2009, prestigious affiliate marketer. Pat Flynn classified affiliate marketer into three kinds — unattached, related and involved — to help separate between affiliate marketer who are intently attached to a product versus the people who are not. Here we'll separate every classification to assist you with concluding which track to take.

1. **Unattached.**

In the unattached busineess deed, the affiliate marketer has no association with the item or administration they are promoting. They have no ability or authority in the specialty of the product, nor might they at any point make claims about its utilization. Normally, an unattached subsidiary will run PPC (pay-per-click) promoting efforts, utilizing a partner connect with the expectation that customers will click it and make a buy all alone.

While unattached affiliate marketing might be appealing because of its absence of commitment, it's by and large for the people who essentially need to create a pay without putting resources into the item or client relationship.

2.   involved

As name indicates, involved affiliate marketing describes those who are intently tied to the product or service they're selling. The affiliate has tested the product themselves, trusts that it will offer an excellent experience and has the authority to make claims about its use, rather than counting on will pay per click. Involved affiliate marketers use their private studies with the product of their advertising efforts, and customers can consider them as dependable sourses of information. Nevertheless, this kind of affiliate marketing requires more legwork and time to construct credibility, however it'll probably bring about extra profits down the road.

How Do affiliate marketers get paid?

A brief and inexpensive approach of making money without the problem of really selling a product, affiliate marketing has an plain draw for those looking to increase their income online. However how an affiliate does receives a commission after linking the seller to the client? the solution can get complicated. The client doesn't constantly want to buy the product for the affiliate to get a kickback, depending on the program, the affiliates contribution to the sellers sales may be measured in another way.

The affiliate may also receive a commission in diverse ways:

1. Pay in line with sale

This is the standard affiliate advertising structure. in this software, the service provider pays the affiliate a percent of the sale fee of the product after the customer purchases the product because of associate advertising and marketing strategies. In different phrases, the affiliate must in reality get the investor to make investments inside the affiliate product before than they are compensated.

2. Pay in keeping with lead

A more complicated system, pay in line with lead affiliate marketing programs compensates the affiliate based on the conversion of leads. The affiliate ought to convince the client to go to the service provider's website and complete the ideal activity — whether or not it's filling out a touch form, signing up for a tribulation of a product, subscribing to a e-newsletter or downloading software program or documents.

3. Pay per click.

Affiliate marketing is largely about producing traffic to websites and trying to get customers to click and take action. So, the parable that affiliate marketing is all just about SEO (search engine optimization) is no surprise. but, at the same time as organic site visitors is at no cost, SEO truly can't sustain affiliate marketers in any such saturated marketplace — which is why a a small number of affiliate marketers utilize PPC.

PPC (pay per click) programs cognizance on incentivizing the affiliate to transmit purchasers from their advertising platform to the merchant's internet site, this indicates the associate ought to interact with the client to the extent that they will pass from the affiliates site to the service provider's web site. The affiliate is paid based on the growth in net visitors.

There are two common standards in PPC:

• CPA (Cost per-acquisition): With this model, the affiliate receives pay whenever the vendor or retailer acquires a lead, of which an affiliate link takes the customer to the service provider's online store and that they take an action, by subscribing to an electronic mail list or filling out a "contact Us" form etc.

• EPC (income-per-click on): this is the degree for the average income in line with a hundred clicks for all affiliates in a store's affiliate software.

4. **Pay per install.**

This payout system is that of which the affiliate gets paid whenever they direct a consumer to the merchant's internet site and installs a product, normally a mobile app or software.

So, if a store budgets for a $0.10 bid for every install generated through an affiliate program, and the campaigns outcome falls around 1,000 installs, then the retailer pays ($0.10 x 1,000) = $100.

Why Be an affiliate Marketer?

1. **Passive earnings**

While any "regular" task calls for you to be at your job to make cash, affiliate ,marketing gives you the potential to make money even as you sleep, through investing some amount of time right into a marketing campaign, you'll see non-stop returns on that time as customers purchase the product over the following days and weeks. You acquire money on your work lengthy after you've completed it. Even while you're no longer in front of your computer, your marketing abilities will continually be bringing in more cash go.

2. **No customer service.**

Individual sellers and organizations offering services or products must address their consumers and make sure they are happy with what they have bought or purchased. Credit to the affiliate marketing structure, you'll never need to be involved with customer service or client satisfaction. The whole task of the affiliate marketer is to link the seller with the customer. The dealer deals with any customer proceedings once you acquire your fee from the sale.

3. **Earn a living from home**

In case you're someone who hates going to the workplace, Affiliate marketing is the right solution. You'll be capable of launching campaigns and getting hold of sales from the products that sellers create while operating from the comfort of your home. This is a job you could do with out ever getting off from your pajamas.

4. **Cost Effective.**

Most businesses require an advance startup costs as well as a cash float to finance the products being offered. However, affiliate advertising and marketing may be accomplished at a low price, meaning you can get started out quick and without much problem. There are no surprising charges to worry about and no need to create a product. starting this line of work is exceedingly uncomplicated.

5. **Handy and flexible.**

Because you're essentially becoming a freelancer, you get optimal independence in putting your own desires, redirecting your route whilst you feel so inclined, deciding on the goods that you are interested in and even determining your very own hours. This therefore means that you could diversify your portfolio if you like or focus completely on easy and direct campaigns. You'll also be free from company regulations and guidelines as well ill-performing teams.

6. **Performance-based rewards**

With other jobs, you can work eighty-hour in a week and nevertheless earn the same salary. The coolest component about affiliate marketing is that it's miles simply based totally for your performance. You'll get from it what you put into it. Honing your reviewing capabilities and writing engaging campaigns will translate to direct upgrades on your revenue. You'll finally receive commission for the extra work you do!

Common Types of Affiliate Marketing Channels

Most affiliates share common practices to ensure that their target audience is engaged and receptive to purchasing promoted products. But not all affiliates advertise the products in the same way. In fact, there are several different marketing channels they may leverage.

1. Influencers.

An influencer is a content creator who holds the power to impact the purchasing decisions of a large segment of the population. This person is in a great position to benefit from affiliate marketing. They already boast an impressive following, so it's easy for them to direct consumers to the seller's products through social media posts, blogs and other interactions with their followers. The influencers then receive a share of the profits they helped to create.

Influencer marketing campaigns are particularly popular on Instagram and TikTok, where brands form partnerships with influencers who are seen as experts or authorities in their specific niches. Depending on the deal, a campaign could consist of a series of product reviews with photos, account takeovers or live videos.

While an influencer might have their own branding and aesthetic, it's important to add elements that tie up with your brand to ensure brand recall and recognition. This can be achieved by using apps like Instasize, where you can quickly edit and customize your campaign's creatives in a tap.

2. Bloggers.

With the ability to rank organically in search engine queries, bloggers excel at increasing a seller's conversions through content marketing. The blogger samples the product or service and then writes a comprehensive review that promotes the brand in a compelling way, driving traffic back to the seller's site. The blogger is awarded for his or her influence spreading the word about the value of the product, helping to improve the seller's sales.

3. **Paid search-focused microsites.**

Developing and monetizing microsites can also garner a serious amount of affiliate sales. These sites are advertised within a partner site or on the sponsored listings of a search engine. They are distinct and separate from the organization's main site. By offering more focused, relevant content to a specific audience, microsites lead to increased conversions due to their simple and straightforward call to action.

4. **Email lists.**

Despite its older origins, email marketing is still a viable source of affiliate marketing income. Some affiliates have email lists they can use to promote the seller's products. Others may leverage email newsletters that include hyperlinks to products, earning a commission after the consumer purchases the product.

Another method is for the affiliate to build an email list over time. They use their various campaigns to collect emails en masse, then send conversion rates, resulting in a top-notch revenue for both the seller and the affiliate. One of the most well known sites is the Amazon affiliate program, Amazon Associates, which boasts the largest market share of affiliate networks (46.15%).

Other big-name affiliate marketing programs include:

- AvantLink.

- LinkConnector.

- CJ Affiliate.

- Affiliate Future.

- ClickBank.

- ShareASale.

- FlexOffers.

Or, if you prefer, you can even reach out to retailers directly and see if they offer an affiliate program. If not, they may still be willing to offer you a special coupon or discount code to share with your audience to help drive traffic to their online shop.

Benefits to Joining the Big Commerce Affiliate Program

1. **Industry-leading Commissions**

In the BigCommerce affiliate program, you receive a 200% bounty per referral and $1,500 per Enterprise referral, with no cap on commissions. Plus, the more referrals you drive through the program, the higher your commission tier will go.

Also, there are no obligations or minimum commitments to join the program.

2. **Strategic Growth.**

Big Commerce provides unique strategies to help you grow, increase your website's visibility and drive more sales. You'll be able to save time and money on content creation by linking to WordPress blogs, webinars and more with quality content developed by BigCommerce for your audience.

3. Powerful Tracking

Our affiliate dashboard offers a broad look at your clicks, trials, sales and commissions. You can view your pay, track metrics and performance and get paid at the same time every month.

4. A Dedicated Account Manager

You will have direct access to an affiliate manager who understands your dealing and your goals. BigCommerce will work with your team and our exchange rate experts to maximize your commissions and pay per click.

Promotion made easy.

In your dashboard, you will have easy contact to our pre-made text links, banners and content. Promote BigCommerce anywhere on your site by simply inserting the affiliate links on your pages.

How to Join The Big Commerce Affiliate Program

If your audience is looking to launch an online business, migrate their ecommerce platform or basically interested in ecommerce content, we encourage you to apply for the BigCommerce affiliate marketing program. Our team will carefully examine your request.

Once approved, you will be given access to support, tracking, reporting, payments and have your own private affiliate link to track every referral you generate. BigCommerce is committed to the success of our affiliate associates.

This is how to build up a site that eventually generates a decent income;

- Keyword Research

- On-Page SEO

- Link Building

- Technical SEO

- Local SEO

- Marketing

- General Marketing

- Content Marketing

- Affiliate Marketing

- Paid Marketing

- Video Marketing

- Data & Studies

Affiliate marketing is a good way to drive sales and generate significant online revenue. Extremely beneficial to both brands and affiliate marketers, the new push toward less traditional out emails regarding the products they are promoting.

5. **Large media websites.**

Designed to create a huge amount of traffic at all times, these sites focus on building an audience of millions. These websites promote products to their massive audience through the use of banners and contextual affiliate links. This method offers superior exposure and improves marketing tactics has certainly paid off.

In fact, affiliate marketing spend in the United States increased from $5.4 billion in 2017 to $8.2 billion in 2022 which means there's plenty of room for those looking to get a piece of the pie.

Tips to Help You Become A Successful Affiliate Marketer

Ready to try your hand on Affiliate Marketing? Here are our top online marketing tips to help you get started. These step-by-step beginner's guide will walk you through how to launch your affiliating marketing business and what benefits you can expect;

1. **Develop a rapport with your audience.**

When beginning your affiliate marketing career, you'll want to cultivate an audience that has very specific interests. This allows you to tailor your affiliate campaigns to that niche, increasing the likelihood that you'll convert. By establishing yourself as an expert in one area instead of promoting a large array of products, you'll be able to market to the people most likely to buy the product.

2. Make it personal.

There is no shortage of products you'll be able to promote. You'll have the ability to pick and choose products that you personally believe in, or even products from your favorite brands, so make sure that your campaigns center around truly valuable products that consumers will enjoy. You'll achieve an impressive conversion rate while simultaneously establishing the reliability of your personal brand.

You'll also want to get really good at email outreach to work with other bloggers and influencers. Use a tool like ContactOut or Voila Norbert to gather people's contact information and send personalized emails to garner guest blogging and affiliate opportunities.

3. Start reviewing products and services.

Focus on surveying products and services that are within your specialty. Then, leveraging the connection you have created with your audience and your stance as an authority, tell your readers why they would benefit from purchasing the product or service you are marketing.

Nearly anything sold online can be reviewed if there is an affiliate program — you can review physical products, digital software or even services booked online, like ride-sharing or travel resort booking. It is especially effective to compare this product to others in the same category. Most importantly, make sure you are generating thorough, articulate content to advance conversions.

4. Use several sources.

Instead of focusing on only an email campaign, also spend time making income with a blog, creating landing pages, posting on survey sites, reaching out to your viewers on social media and even looking into cross-channel promotions.

Test a range of digital marketing strategies to see which one your readers responds to the most. Make frequent use of this modus operandi.

5. Choose campaigns with care.

No matter how excellent your online marketing skills are, you'll make less income on a bad product than you will on a legiit one. Take the time to review the demand for a new product before promoting it. Make sure to research the seller with care before teaming up. Your time is significance, and you want to be sure you're spending it on a product that is lucrative and a seller you can trust in.

6. Stay current with trends.

There is a stern competition in the affiliate marketing sphere. You'll want to make sure you stay on zenith of any new trends to ensure you remain competitive. Additionally, you'll likely be able to benefit from at least a few of the new marketing techniques that are frequently being produced. Be sure you're keeping up to date on all these new strategies to guarantee that your exchange rates, and therefore revenue, will be as high as possible.

Conclusively, Affiliate marketing is an elegantly direct process, affiliate marketing through reviews, blogs, social media, webinar software and other platforms is a new frontier in marketing that's just waiting to be utilized. No affiliate marketing wheels were reinvented here. These are the nitty-gritty, and applying them will get you off on the right foot. Just don't expect life-changing income or the freedom to quit your 9-5 overnight. Affiliate marketing takes time. Focus firstly on making your first affiliate sale. As your site grows, set new goals, and continue experimenting.

Follow the tips included in this section, and you'll be able to engage your audience, convert passive readers into active clients and enhance your proceeds one click at a time.

CHAPTER FIVE
WORKING AS A VIRTUAL ASSISTANT (VA)

Bloggers and online entrepreneurs could continuously utilize some assistance and that is where you come in as a virtual assistant. Normally a genuinely simple occupation should be possible from home you'll have to accomplish some administrator work and post via social media; however you can likewise go about as customer care. The particular set of working responsibilities relies upon your manager's requirements - you'll do anything that they need most right now for their business to easily work. For this reason you ought to initially investigate the field and conclude regardless of whether you need to get into it, and afterward see specific bids for employment and plan for your desired ones to apply for. You can look for VA occupations on the very sites that propose independent work, some of which I referenced in the independent composing segment. Menial helpers offer help to organizations and people from a distance. This is one of the top work from home open doors you can begin your own with practically zero forthright venture. There are various virtual assistants administrations you can propose to procure a consistent pay.

What do Virtual Assistants do?

A virtual assistant occupation can shift contingent upon their abilities and target clients. A few virtual assistants work on unambiguous undertakings like plan or promoting, while others offer more broad administrations. A fruitful VA is one that is keen on independent work and offering incredible support to clients.

Common Tasks Of A Virtual Assistant

Menial helpers can deal with an enormous cluster of administrations for their clients. Here are a few errands you might deal with:

- Information passage

- Authoritative undertakings like getting sorted out computerized records

- Inbox management

- Booking

- Client assistance

- Social media management like booking and answering requests

- Internet promoting

- Writing for a blog

- Blog remarking

- Drafting and sending official statements

- Editing and altering

- Visual depiction

- Web improvement

- Accounting

- Investigating and research

What amount do **Virtual Assistants** Procure Each Hour?

Numerous virtual assistants work at an hourly rate. Others get compensated for finishing explicit responsibilities. Also, some even charge month to month or yearly rates. Pay differs emphatically based on abilities and administrations offered. Since you're in fact an entrepreneur in the event that you become a virtual assistants, you're responsible for setting rates all alone. Notwithstanding, VA's report acquiring a normal of $19.46 each hour. Also, section level VAs might hope to procure about $15 each hour.

What do a **virtual assistants** Make Each Year?

Virtual assistants pay rates shift in light of what administrations you give, how long you work, and your abilities and experience. Assuming you have a sought after specialty or have broad experience, take part in compensation exchange to get your optimal rate. Menial helper compensations frequently fall around $37,023.

Bringing In Cash As A **Virtual Assistants**

If you have any desire to bring in cash as a VA, here are a few choices for beginning your own web-based business.

1. Secure One Virtual assistant Position

To keep it basic and bring in only a tad of cash, get a new line of work posting and apply similarly as you would with customary business. This would essentially be an agreement opportunity and you could partake in an adaptable timetable and remote work.

2. Independent with Different Clients

On the other hand, you can work with more than one client to bring in significantly more cash. This may likewise call for greater investment or permit you to work with organizations that need assistance with only a couple of undertakings every week.

3. Offer Various Administrations

A few VA's essentially act as a clerical specialist, taking care of a variety of errands. This might assist you with engaging all the more new clients. However, it likewise requires a more extensive exhibit of abilities.

4. Make a Specialty

A few VAs rather center around only one region, such as overseeing online entertainment accounts or answering client requests. This can assist you with restricting a main interest group and spotlight on the things you're best at.

5. Work with an Office

There are VA offices and occupation sheets that can assist you with tracking down work. They might take a cut of each position or charge an expense. In any case, it might assist you with tracking down additional potential open doors.

6. Interface with Other Online Organizations

When you thin down the kind of entrepreneur you serve, track down other internet based experts with similar objective clients. For instance, assuming you offer email showcasing the executives, allude clients to those that deal content creation administrations. You might get an additional references and offer significantly more benefit to clients.

7. Market to Nearby Organizations

Numerous VA's get clients on the web. However, you can likewise advertise locally assuming that is your specialty. Promote in nearby distributions or meet entrepreneurs at neighborhood occasions to offer administrations.

8. Request References

When you work for certain clients, request that they allude others in their industry to acquire significantly more business. Tributes can likewise help.

How to Get Started With Your Virtual Assistant Business

Functioning as a VA or online individual colleague implies maintaining your own business. In any case, you just need a couple of nuts and bolts to get everything rolling as a section level Virtual assistant, similar to an internet connection and computer or laptop. Notwithstanding, it is critical to ask how does a VA respond? Here are other moves toward bringing the method for augmenting month to month pay:

1. Take a virtual assistant instructional class:

VAs don't require formal training. However, you might in any case profit from instructional classes to assist you with building hierarchical abilities or acquire explicit devices like email promoting programming.

2. Choose what administrations to offer:

Consider in the event that you're ready to deal with a variety of undertakings like a web-based chief colleague or on the other hand on the off chance that you'd prefer center around a particular region like overseeing blog entry content and making a publication schedule.

3. Set rates:

At this point, decide the amount you're ready to charge for each contribution. Peruse VA destinations to get familiar with the going rate. However, you might charge more in the event that you have broad experience or heaps of interest.

4. Find menial helper occupations:

Many organizations enlist menial helpers as they would different laborers. Check your #1 quest for new employment site to secure menial helper positions in your specialty. You can likewise check Facebook gatherings and neighborhood work sheets. Essentially, investigate how to view as a remote helper so you can make yourself accessible there.

5. Create a web-based presence:

A few organizations might need to see social verification to dive more deeply into precisely exact thing you offer. Your own site and online entertainment stages can assist you with appearing to be more trustworthy.

6. Market your administrations:

You might try and make deals pages and online advertisements to attract more possible clients.

7. Set your own hours:

Heaps of individuals are keen on becoming VAs since they're the absolute most adaptable positions around. Figure out what hours you can work in view of family and different responsibilities and afterward convey that to likely clients.

Step by step instructions to Amplify Your Income from **virtual assistant** Occupations

The pay you acquire while initially beginning your VA business may not be the most amazing job you could ever imagine compensation. Be that as it may, the accompanying tips can assist you with procuring more:

- Arrange compensations and rates: You don't need to take the principal offer. Request what you need, and express no to open doors that don't fit.

- Robotize tedious undertakings: You can accomplish more in the event that you save time on administrator errands like invoicing. Put resources into computerization apparatuses to remove these things.

- Focus on top clients: Assuming you have sufficient work to keep occupied, begin expressing no to low paying position and spotlight on those that pay the most.

- Foster new abilities: You can charge more assuming you have popular abilities. So learn new stages and programming that your clients esteem.

- Raise rates occasionally: Whenever you've been doing business for a little while, you have more insight. Charge appropriately.

Most virtual assistant don't get rich immediately, however procuring a nice income is conceivable. Those with essential abilities and simply a client or two may procure a couple hundred bucks each month. In any case, those with significant level abilities, long stretches of involvement, and a few clients can procure $100,000 each year or more.

Chapter Six

Sell Physical Products Online

Another way to earn money online is by selling physical products on sites like Amazon and eBay. While you may not earn enough to make a living selling your own personal items (unless you are able to acquire a lot of goods at low costs and can turn them around quickly), you can also help others sell their things, thereby earning yourself a nice little commission in the process. If you're highly creative, have a side hobby, and/or are very good at a particular handicraft, then it's not a bad idea to invest in it and try selling your creations online. Whether it's handmade soaps, handmade candles, handmade jewelry, T-shirts, shawls, other pieces of clothing, mugs, or illustrations – whatever it is, there is a place on the internet for it.

Nowadays, there are plenty of online stores and platforms on which you can sell your handmade products, including Etsy, Amazon Handmade, Ruby Lane, Aftcra (for US users only), and Folksy (for UK users only) .Great news if you want to start an online shop, you can do it for free! Here are the best free e-commerce website builders in 2022. There are also platforms that allow you to create your own store at an affordable price, such as Shopify, Squarespace, Wix, and others. What I'm basically trying to say here is there are a lot of opportunities out there. You can also earn money by launching a dropshipping store, where you won't need to handle the product directly. This way, you'll be an affiliate to another brand, business, or creative individual.

How To Get Started

How do you get started selling? Here are a few simple steps:

1. **Find a product to sell.**

Your first step to making this Internet option work is finding a product to sell. Fortunately, there are several ways to go about it. For instance, you can start by taking a look around your house and seeing what you have that you no longer want or need as selling your unwanted or unused items is a great way to get them out of your house without just sending them to the trash. The key to making a lot of money is to make sure they are still in good, if not excellent condition. That being said, some people do sell broken things online as others may be buying them with the intent of fixing them and offering them for resale. So, in essence, nothing is off limits ("one man's junk is another man's treasure") as long as you are honest and market it accordingly.

A second option is to frequent yard and garage sales (and swap meets, flea markets, and antique sales), as sometimes you can find great deals there that you can resell online. Whether the item you purchased is in great condition already or you have what it takes to refinish it, you can make a lot of money off other people's no longer wanted goods. If you can find a really good deal at retail or even wholesale stores, you can also buy direct from them and resell the items at a higher price. Liquidation events, going out of business sales, and discontinued items are great for this purpose. Just be aware that buying items with the sole purpose of resale may require that you pay tax on them, so you may want to consult with an accountant before taking that route.

Good items to consider selling are ones that appeal to a niche market. Hobbyists like to find unique things online, making this one area that you can do really well in. Still not sure what to sell? EBay has a Selling Inspiration House that can help you "find top-selling items in your home." Just pick a room, select an item, and it will tell you how much they are currently going for online.

2. Pick a platform and create an account

Now that you have something to sell, it is time to decide where it is you want to sell it. Two of the most notable sites are Amazon and eBay. However, you can also list your item on Craigslist (best for bigger items like cars and furniture). Be sure to read each one carefully so you know up front what is required of you as a seller and how much commission they will take on the sale. Some charge you to a subscription fee as well, so you're going to want to check all of this out prior to signing up. Whichever one you choose, you're going to have to create an account in order to list and get paid. So, pick the one (or ones) that is best suited for you and the items you want to get rid of, and provide all of the requested information to create a complete account.

In order to get your money from them, you are also going to have to provide payment information. To keep your bank information private, you can always create a PayPal account and accept payment that way. (PayPal does charge fees as well, so you may have to weigh that into the cost and whether or not it is worth it given what you are selling.) A great way to figure out which site you prefer is to buy something from it before even placing your goods for sale. This way you get firsthand knowledge of how it works from the buyer's perspective, allowing you to take them into consideration when it comes to selling your goods online.

3. Prepare your listing for optimal results

To get good results on your listing, you want to include both benefits and features of your product. For example, features of a TV include screen size, resolution, and things like that, whereas benefits are being able to see the television clearer, having a flat-screen that doesn't take up too much room, and being able to see your favorite sports up close, almost as if you were there in person. Your product description needs to be complete as well. The more information you provide about what it is you're selling, the easier it will be for people to determine if that is what they are looking for. Think like a buyer and include everything you would want to know if you were making the purchase yourself.

It helps to be familiar with jargon that is often used on popular selling sites. For example, BN stands for brand new and VTG means vintage. HTF represents a hard to find item and VGC tells the buyer it is in very good condition. If something is unique or distinct about your product, point it out. The more you can make your product a "one of a kind," the greater your chance of selling it. Use keywords in your listing so that your product can be easily found by anyone searching for it. Not sure which ones to use? Consider what words you would use to search for the item and just use them. Include the brand if it is likely to make a difference.

Your product pictures (the more the better) need to be high quality. If they are fuzzy or too far away, you're not going to give prospective buyers a good feeling. Also, make sure the surrounding environment is good too because people like to buy from others who appear to take care of their things. If you're stuck on any of these things, look up other people's listings and use them as templates to write yours. Just be sure to choose a top seller so that you know how to create an ad that sells, not one that doesn't get noticed.

4. **Set your price**

As far as price is concerned, this one may take a little bit of research. Google the item you are selling and see what others are getting for it. Before pricing yours though, you'll want to take into consideration its condition. Depending on the site you intend to use, you can sell your item via traditional auction or by set price. Auction means that you sell to the highest bidder (and you may want to set a minimum price so you don't practically give it away) and set price means that you sell it to anyone that wants it for the price which you are selling it. If you have a bunch of smaller items and don't want to price them for individual sale, you may want to group them together and sell them as a package. This may also entice a buyer as they will be getting several things for one standard rate.

An additional tip: some successful sellers offer free shipping as it catches people's attention. It's easy enough do as you just have to add this amount to your base price. The one caveat is that shipping isn't always going to be the same price as it is location dependent. So, you're going to want to keep this in mind if you choose to take this route.

5. **List your product on Amazon or eBay**

When you decide to list your product, you'll want to time your listing so you get the most out of it. For example, if you only have a 10-day window, you may want to post your product on a Thursday so that it appears online for two full weekends, giving you more bangs for your buck. Another factor to consider is whether your item is seasonal, or in high demand during certain times of the year. If this is the case, you may want to wait to sell it, drawing in the most money possible.

6. **Promote your product**

Share your product on your social media sites, website, in forums, or on any other Internet site you can think of to draw attention to it. You never know. Even if the people you're reaching out to have no interest in it, they might know someone who does and share it with them. It's a win-win!

7. Make the deal

Once you have a specific buyer, you're ready to close the deal. This is a great time to confirm things such as price and delivery, as well as answer any questions they may have. This is also where you collect payment. It is very important that you do this prior to shipping your item so that you don't wind up sending it out and never getting the money, in return.

8. Deliver your product

You want to make sure your item arrives in the same condition it left you in, so you're going to want to pack it well. Do this by putting in extra padding to avoid unintentional breakage or damage by the shipping company. You can even go one step further and take pictures of your item as it is being packaged as well as the finished box to show what condition it was in when it left you. Then ship it according to the site's requirements, being sure to get a tracking number and insurance if you want to be extra safe or the item is worth a lot of money. Having your buyer sign for it ensures that they received it, and it protects you from scammers who insist that it never arrived.

9. Grow your product-based business

In order to survive long-term and grow on sites like eBay, you need to get good feedback from the people that you sell to. Keep this in mind as every interaction you have with your customers has the potential to promote your business—or break it. Staying in good contact with them every step of the way will help establish a good buyer/seller relationship. Check your email often and don't list things while you're going to be away for an extended period of time as it could look bad on you as a seller.

As the Internet has evolved and eCommerce and delivery systems have improved, more retailers have decided to sell their physical products over the internet and make money selling online. Setting up an online store that sells physical items is a relatively easy and affordable way to start an online business, and you could be selling your products pretty quickly to a local and worldwide market.

If you're not sure how to sell physical items online, you may get inspiration from the list below;

1. **Third Party Ecommerce Systems**

If you want another company to take care of the technical side of your online business, you have a wide range of third-party shopping systems like Shopify to choose from. There are numerous **Shopify reviews** that will explain why it's such a popular eCommerce platform. Third-party systems are usually extremely secure and they are updated on a regular basis by the security team of the company you are dealing with. You can easily change the look of your website and add products. You are normally charged a monthly or annual fee to set up shop, but it's well worth the money.

2. **Set Up Your Own Ecommerce Store**

If you are able to store your own products and fulfill online orders, you may be in a position to set up your own ecommerce store on your own **domain and hosting platform**. There are many shopping systems available that allow you to display your products, take orders, process payments and fulfill each order taken through your website.

With these systems, you have total control of them and you can make changes to these systems whenever you wish. However, you need to keep your **ecommerce** system maintained and secure with the latest security updates.

3. Dropshipping

Dropshipping is an extremely popular and straightforward way to sell physical products through another company. Your online store sells the physical item and this product is bought from a dropshipping company at a reduced price. The product is then shipped to your customer by the dropshipping company. Your profit is the difference between the price you charge your customer for the item sold and the price the dropshipper charges you to fulfill the order.

4. Auction Websites

Since eBay was established, a huge number of <u>auction websites</u> have emerged. They can be a great place to pick up a bargain if you're a shopper, and these websites are also the perfect places to sell all kinds of physical items because thousands of shoppers flock to auction websites every day.

5. Amazon and Other Leading Marketplaces

Sometimes it pays to piggyback off the popularity of other websites, instead of going it alone. Many of the world's biggest marketplaces like **Amazon** allow retailers to sell their products on these huge websites. In some cases, these companies even store and fulfill all of your orders, so that you can focus on promoting your products to more shoppers and customers.

Conclusively, It's never been as easy as it is now to set up an online store, **Ecommerce** technologies keep improving and more shoppers want to buy items online, so you should seriously consider each of the options above.

The Ultimate Guide

CHAPTER SEVEN
CREATE ONLINE COURSES

Offering online courses is similar to coaching, which means you need to have a deeper understanding of a certain topic or a set of skills. With the requirements for social distancing and the overall anxiety the pandemic has set off, online courses have become a way for people to keep learning and stay connected, which means your expertise is likely to be much more appreciated nowadays. People go online for a variety of reasons, including entertainment and socializing. But the Internet is also used to find information and learn new things. Not sure how to use a new piece of software? There is probably a video tutorial on YouTube. Want to know what you can make for lunch with the few ingredients you have in your fridge? Check Pinterest for a recipe.

This need for information and instruction has created a great opportunity for you to get paid for your knowledge. While some people have done this by creating a blog or writing books, an online course is another method of selling what you know. Many people don't think they know enough about a topic to teach it, but the truth is, you don't have to be an expert to create and sell an online course. You simply need to know more than most. The topics you can cover are vast including art or photography, personal development, music, gardening, cooking, marketing, technology, language, and more. Many people have made thousands of dollars a month with online courses teaching things like, how to play the guitar, how to use specific software, or how to bake bread.

There are plenty of websites out there that will help you set up your own online course. Some of the best are:

- **Udemy** – Arguably the most well-known site for online courses, Udemy gives you a vast space in which you can show your talents and expertise.

- **Teachable** – This is a site that allows you to create your very own online courses and offer coaching services. Teachable even offers you a free webinar so you can learn how to get started faster.

- **SkillShare** – SkillShare is another great site that offers lots of categories to people who want to teach online and eager students alike!

Before you dive in and start creating your own online course, it helps to look at the pros and cons to see if this is the right avenue for you to pursue.

Pros and cons of creating online courses

Pros:

- Easy-to-use platforms have simplified online course creation

- You can offer courses that complement your existing business

- Create passive income by re-selling the same online course continually

- Use an online course to lead customers to your other product offerings

- Online availability brings in clients from all over the globe

Cons:

- Online courses can be time-consuming to create

- Depending on the platform you choose, products may not be hosted on your own website

- Courses are typically only successful if you target what's already selling

- Finding the pricing sweet spot can be challenging

Pros:

Several new online course platforms are available to make setting up and selling your course easier than ever. Additionally, due to continually advancing technology, many of the tools and equipment needed to create a course are very simple to use, with professional-quality results. You can create courses to sell as an addition to your existing business. For example, if you're a blogger, you can offer a course that delves deeper into something specific in your blog's topic area. If you offer a service, you can design and offer an online course for people who would rather learn and do the work on their own instead of hiring you.

Creating and selling online courses can offer you a passive income stream. You only have to create a course once, and then you can sell it over and over. Additionally, because your course is online, you can have students from all over the world, in any time zone, without any additional effort. One of the creative ways to use an online course for marketing purposes is to use it as part of a funnel system to lead students to your coaching program or other services. You can give them a small amount of information or teach them a basic-level service, and then direct them to your other paid offerings if they want more of what you have to offer.

Cons

Quality online courses usually offer students a variety of content delivery methods such as text and video, which can take time to create. Users expect to be able to have the course in a format to access on their phone or laptop, with video and audio files so they can watch or listen on their daily commute, for example. When designing your online course, you'll need to choose an online service to host your finished product. This could be your own website, or it could be a hosted service such as Udemy. Keep in mind that if you choose Udemy or a similar site, you don't "own" the market or the platform, Udemy does.

Like all other money-making ventures, your success depends on the need or desire for your course, and your ability to attract your target market. It's worth putting the time into keyword and trend research to focus on what's trending now and what people want to buy. It can be a challenge to correctly price your course to maximize your income while still making it affordable for students. This part takes some trial and error and also involves looking at comparable online courses and getting an estimate of the market's going rate vs. the amount you want to charge.

How to Create an Online Course

If you're ready to delve into the world of online teaching, follow the steps below.

1. Choose a Course Topic

Make a list of things you know about. Perhaps it's something your friends and family ask you for help on. Maybe it's a skill related to your job (i.e., how to use Evernote or how to be productive working at home). Do you have a hobby you can teach others about, such as watercolor painting for beginners or how to lower your score in golf?

2. Do Market Research

You don't want to spend a lot of time creating a course that no one will buy. Many people might want to know about your topic, but the question is; are they willing to pay to learn it? Before you invest time in your course, research who the best buyer for it would be, and whether or not they're ready, willing and able to buy it.

3. Outline Your Course

If you've determined there is a market willing to buy your course, the next step is in determining what you'll put in the course. By the nature of a course, the content you provide should go deep into the topic and cover all important aspects. A course isn't like a blog post, which often just skims the surface.

To help organize your course, think in terms of modules and lessons. A module would be the overall subtopic, with the lessons providing the details of that subject. For example, if you have a course on starting a home business, you might have a module on business plans. Your lessons in that module would include "How to determine your USP" and "How to identify your target market."

4. Decide the Best Methods to Deliver Your Lessons

There is an expectation that online courses will offer a variety of teaching methods, such as text, video, worksheets, checklists, infographics, audio, and anything else that delivers information.

The trick is in determining what format is best for what you're trying to teach. In some cases, you might offer two methods for one lesson. For example, if you were teaching a course on how to use Quickbooks, you might have both a step-by-step text instruction and a video tutorial on how to install and set up the software.

5. Create Your Lessons

It is the most time-consuming aspect of creating an online course. Consider creating a logo or a color theme that appears in all lesson content. Proofread your text lessons and watch your videos to make sure there are no errors or glitches.

6. Determine How You'll Sell Your Lesson

For the most control, create a website to host and deliver your lesson. There are membership site scripts and WordPress plugins that can help you set up a system for selling and delivering your course. For faster, less technical effort, you can use an online course service, such as Udemy or SkillShare. Pay from these sites varies. For example, Udemy's instructor pay depends on how the sale was generated (through its marketplace, an affiliate, or directly from you).

The benefit to these resources is that you simply upload your course and the sites take care of selling it to their members/market, including payment processing. The downside is that they own the market and platform. Plus, you're competing with other course providers, which can mean the need to reduce the price of your course to compete.

A final option is a service such as Teachable or Ruzuku, both of which offer some of the benefits of self-hosted with the ease and speed of Udemy. These options have easy creation and upload like the course service marketplaces, but you can add your own domain, and customize your school like in self-hosted options. Some offer their resources for free, with more bells and whistles with paid plans. Most integrate with PayPal, or you can use their payment service.

Most of the above options don't require exclusivity so that you can sell your course on more than one platform. Even so, be sure to read the terms of service before offering your course on multiple platforms.

7. Load Your Course Online

Once you've picked your platform, upload your course. If the platform allows you to customize your course, such as adding a logo or color scheme, add them. It will help you create your unique brand.

8. Market Your Course

Regardless of your platform, you need to promote your course. Even using a service like Udemy, in which students can find you by perusing the Udemy marketplace, you want to do your own marketing.

Start by creating a marketing plan that includes who your market is, where you can find them, and how you can entice them to check out your course. Great course marketing options include social media, PPC advertising, such as Facebook ads, and article marketing. There are many other free and low-cost marketing options as well.

9. Keep Your Course Information Up-to-Date

Every few months or so, check that your course information is current and relevant. Outdated information doesn't help your students and can lead to bad reviews. Don't forget to check and fix any broken links to resources.

10. Rinse and Repeat

There's no rule that you have to stick with one course. If there are other courses you can teach related to your initial course, create those. You can then refer your students to these other courses. For example, if you offer a course on how to write a mystery, you can add a course on how to publish a book and/or how to market a book. You can also create new courses in completely different areas.

Conclusively, Creating and selling online courses can be quite lucrative if you're able to provide a great course and reach your target marketing. Plus, with easier to use and more affordable resources to host your course, there's no reason to avoid becoming an online instructor. While it can take time to create all the lessons in your course, once uploaded, it can become a profitable source of passive income to your existing business or as a business all on its own.

CHAPER EIGHT
LAUNCHING A PODCAST

Podcasts have become one of the most famous sorts of web content, particularly among youthful people. Specialists foresee that there will be 140 million digital recording audience members in the US in 2022. Obviously, that number is supposed to develop without further ado, hitting 164 million out of 2024. On the off chance that you're positive about your correspondence, sound altering, and web-based entertainment the board abilities, beginning a digital broadcast may be great for you. To build your opportunities for progress, you'll need to put resources into quality sound hardware, recording programming, and webcast facilitating, as well as foster a miniature specialty idea.

Why make an effort not to market to everybody? Basically in light of the fact that general digital recording subjects won't assist you with building a following as you will not have the option to contact many individuals through all the commotion on the web. Tracking down the right point for your podcast is definitely not a simple undertaking as it must be sufficiently tight to suck individuals in, yet wide enough to permit you to record heaps of episodes. In the event that you just can't think of any smart thoughts, you should begin with a general rundown and afterward pick your #1 points and limited them down into miniature specialties.

Do-It-Yourself instructional exercises, tech surveys, computer game audits, sustenance and explicit weight control plans, have driven exercise meetings, directed reflections, book proposals and studies, and elective residing (van life, minimalistic houses, off-framework residing, and so on) are just a portion of the endless webcast subjects you can consider gaining practical experience in. Alright, yet how might I bring in cash? Indeed, until you acquire the trust of your audience members, partner promoting will be the most secure method for adapting your web recording. When your crowd arrives at huge number of audience members, you'll have the option to bring in cash by making a Patreon page.

Motivations to send off a Podcast:

•	As shown by Measurements, 57% of Americans have waited there, paying attention to a sound computerized broadcast;

•	Right when gotten along admirably, podcasting makes different shocking online business open entryways, including getting allies and marketing experts, changing episodes into blog passages, selling your things/organizations, making significant affiliations; and

•	Your Digital broadcast group won't hear messages from your opponents (web recording exclusivity).

Guidelines to Begin a Digital recording: All that You Want to Be aware to Succeed

"Be clear about the things that are fundamental for you," maker and nonconformist Karen Walrond once communicated. Moreover, what's an unrivaled strategy for voicing your perspective and deal your understanding than by starting a webcast? By building trust, exhibiting authority, and drawing in crowd individuals, a webcast is a convincing strategy for getting your name and brand out there. Exactly when you make a site, for example, showing your show with a Web recording Player is a staggering technique for driving more traffic to your website and attract new clients. This all out helper will walk you through how to start a computerized broadcast. We'll begin with helping you with picking your point and webcast plan, then, move into equipment, recording, and the dispersing framework. Eventually, we'll dive into the best ways of publicizing and adjust your advanced recording.

The disrepute of digital recordings

To some degree as of late webcast, throng of individuals have duplicated and 57% of U.S. clients focus on computerized communicates regularly. This basic addition can be cleared up by the computerized recording's useful limit with regards to be focused on in a rush. Because of this wonderful benefit, when people find a show they're related with, they're most likely going to become undaunted crowd individuals. In any case, there's as yet a lot of unseen space in this creating news source. While there are 600 million locales and 37 million YouTube channels on the web, there are somewhere near 2 million advanced accounts. Along these lines, if you're contemplating starting a web recording, right now's the chance to take a cut of the pie — before the resistance increases.

Step By Step Directions To Start A Computerized Recording

Preparing

1. Comprehend what compelss a good computerized Webcast

2. Set forth your targets

3. Pick your topic

4. Describe your interested party

5. Name your computerized Digital broadcast

6. Pick your show plan

7. Choose your commonplace episode length

Planning

8. Script your show

9. Get ready

10. Select your advanced Web recording music

11. Plan your show's cover workmanship

12. Welcome computerized Digital recording guests

Recording and Altering

13. Find a spot to record

14. Use the right mouthpiece techniques

15. Record far off guests or co-has

16. Work with adjusting programming

Launching

17. Pick a computerized broadcast facilitating with site

18. Make a site for your computerized Web recording

19. Make a portrayal for your webcast

20. Title your episodes

21. Present your show to advanced broadcast lists

Promoting and turning into your computerized broadcast

22. Execute a web recording advancing procedure

23. Keep people tuning in

24. Adjust your web recording

25. Circulate new fulfilled regularly

Preparing

1. Comprehend what constrains a fair Digital recording

As you begin anticipating your podcasting adventure, it's crucial to make a webcast thought and pick a subject that will put you in a decent position. To do this, first, explore what the best podcasters share for all intents and purposes:

- They are fiery about their subject

- They stick to a specific subject or subject

- They recollect their crowd individuals and reliably plan to give them regard

- They are unsurprising in their course of action and circulating arrangement

- They add a singular touch to isolate themselves

We ought to explore a veritable model. The Joe Rogan Experience is one of the most notable web accounts that exist today, with a normal 11 million crowd individuals for every episode. However, why is his web recording so viable? Crowd individuals are attracted to

Rogan's suggestion since they acknowledge he is unimaginably intriguing, well disposed, and, for certain, locking in.

2. Set forth your targets

At the point when you know why you really want to start a web recording, the rest will be much more clear. Your inspiration might be to enlighten, persuade or lock in. For example, these rousing web accounts have the sensible goal of moving crowd individuals.

While working with an assistant or co-have, you ought to portray your positions and suppositions without skipping a beat. For example, presume that one of you is responsible for modifying the sound, and the other is liable for managing the virtual diversion accounts. The earlier you set forth these targets for every closely involved individual, the better.

3. Pick your point

Do you end up returning once more and analyzing comparable focuses at social affairs, feasts, and other parties? Whether it's Bitcoin, Keto eating less low quality food, or legislative issues, you presumably have two or three subjects you're both excited about and have the ability or data to inspect. Endeavor to pinpoint something you can discuss for 50+ episodes, and ideally, you can progress in that subject with subtopics. For example, business computerized broadcasts can isolate their substance into subtopics like undertaking, starting a business, and productivity tips.

Expecting you wish to pick a webcast point considering interest, Statista found that satire (22%) is the super computerized keep sort in the U.S. After the parody, the top webcast orders are news (21%), certifiable bad behavior (18%), and sports (17%). Remember, you don't must have a Ph.D. around here, nor do you really want to masterfully be related with it. It's more ordinary than you make sure to start a computerized recording associated with side endlessly interests. Take a gander at these innovative computerized recording subjects to help you with creating your idea.

4. Describe your vested party

That is the very thing they say if your group is everyone, your group is no one. Hence it's fundamental to change an end group to the subject you choose to start a computerized broadcast about. By outlining your optimal crowd and tending to the requests under, you can make huge substance that keeps people partook in your show:

- Who is your fragment?

- Which issues do they face concerning your topic?

- What do they have to learn?

- How should your computerized broadcast help them?

- Where are they contributing their energy on the web?

- How should you keep them secured?

We support anyone starting a web recording to write these reactions down. Castos has made this steady design that licenses you to describe your ideal crowd.

5. Name your Podcast

Your webcast name can play a tremendous figure its thriving. With a sound and illustrative webcast name, you could even more at any point successfully get found, stick out, and specifically — be reviewed. There are different perspectives of a web recording name. One procedure is to plug expressions associated with your point into a name generator instrument. Then again, you can use these comparable watchwords and preliminary with different naming conditions. Guarantee you pick a name that is somewhat greater than your topic. Thusly, you're not encased and can stretch out past your specialty expecting you decide to.

At times, the best computerized broadcast names are a piece out-of-the-holder, so give yourself creative freedom. Wix actually started a web recording called What's the deal? — whose name begins from the prerequisite for business visionaries and creative trailblazers to create and really focus on what's coming immediately constantly. Whenever you've picked your name, ensure that it's not as of now used on computerized broadcast vaults like Spotify and Mac Digital recordings. Then, at that point, check whether the space name is at this point open, this will be huge when you make a website for your web recording later on.

6. Pick your show plan

You can peruse moving web recording plans for your show. The huge thing is to keep it consistent, so your throng of individuals understand what the future holds as they continue to tune in. Coming up next are five of the most notable plans:

• Interview: The host of a gathering computerized broadcast will dependably invite significant guests to their show and work with a conversation with them. This is the most notable advanced recording plan and is useful for getting new crowd individuals as guests can get new groups and transparency. Additionally, it's moreover an amazing technique for talking with charming people you regard. In any case, consider that you believe should do a work and meaning to set up your gatherings.

- Solo show: A presentation or talk style computerized recording is one in which a singular host addresses the term of the show. The benefit is that you can work independently, while the potential test is that you're the only one talking f as long as necessary.

- Co-facilitated: A conversational digital recording where at least two hosts can run thoughts by one another. This organization is brilliant for discussing, great chat and comedy.

- Panel: This web recording design is a roundtable conversation where a few speakers give their feedback and conclusions regarding a matter. An advantage for the audience is that they can hear numerous different points of view on a solitary episode.

- Prearranged narrating digital broadcasts: These can either be fiction or true to life shows that have a solitary subject and a few stories inside that theme. Here you will frequently find narrative style shows, including docu-dramatizations.

7. Decide your typical episode length

After you've concluded which webcast design you're intending to work with, consider to your episode length. With a steady length, you'll have a more expert show that audience members are know about, and they can carve out the best opportunity to accommodate your webcast into their timetable.

Digital broadcasts can go somewhere in the range of five minutes to six hours. While there is no ideal webcast length, many individuals go for the gold moment episodes to line up with normal drive times. Truth be told, Buzzsprout observed that 20-40 minutes is the most widely recognized episode length, with 31% falling into this reach. The second most famous digital recording length is 40-an hour which applies to 22% of webcast episodes.

Preparing

8. Script your show

With a strong show diagram and general content close by, you'll have the option to record effortlessly and save time arranging every episode. We don't mean composing a full paper and perusing it in exactly the same words — all things considered, use list items and a steady request for key components, for example, presenting the show's point, the questioner (if pertinent) and having a rundown toward the end.

Here is an illustration of a show frame:

- Introduction music: Begin your webcast with a signature tune to start off the episode.

- Episode presentation: Present yourself, your digital recording name and what's going on with your show. Then, at that point, give a concise rundown of what audience members will escape the present episodes. Keep in mind, the initial 5 minutes are significant for establishing a decent first connection as 20-35% of audience members will generally drop off on the off chance that they don't see esteem by then.

- Visitor introduction (if relevant): Offer your visitor's name and add some setting in regards to their experience and skill. Make it clear to audience members why this visitor is on your show and what they can gain from that person.

- Episode fundamental substance: Talk about the episode's subjects exhaustively. Whether it's a meeting, story, news update or speech — this is the episode's meat. Go ahead and incorporate a promotion opening here toward the beginning, center or end.

- Wrap up: Sum up the critical focal points from today and thank any visitors you could have had on the show. Additionally, thank your audience members for tuning in. This can likewise be an incredible time for reporting impending occasions, episodes or seasons.

- Inspire: This is your opportunity to request that audience members buy in, survey or share your digital recording. Try not to avoid this part, as those activities can essentially work on your number of audience members.

- Outro music: Play a consummation melody to represent your episode has wrapped up.

9. Get furnished with a mouthpiece

At the point when you start a webcast, you don't have to put resources into broad hardware, however one energetically suggested thing is a quality receiver. USB receivers are the most well known to utilize and can arrive in a great many costs. We've explored the market and found these are the top-suggested receivers for podcasting:

- Sound Technica ATR2100x-USB Receiver

- Samson Q2U Receiver

- Rode Podcaster USB Dynamic Receiver

On top of your mic, you could likewise need to get soundproof earphones, a mic arm and a shock mount (these forestall undesirable development of your receiver and let you place the mouthpiece in an ideal position).

10. Select your digital recording music

It's generally expected practice to open your episodes with a signature melody and end with an outro tune. You can find a melody that accommodates your show utilizing eminence free music on destinations like Bensound, Premium Beat, and Sound Wilderness. Whenever you've picked your subject, download it to your PC. In the altering and recording stage, you will transfer it into your product.

11. Plan your show's cover workmanship

Making an outwardly engaging workmanship cover is a fundamental stage in knowing how to begin a digital broadcast. Cover craftsmanship is the little square picture seen close to your web recording name on places like Spotify or your site. This visual ought to impart the subject of your digital broadcast. By and large, particulars require a cover picture to be a JPG or PNG record that is 3000 x 3000 pixels and has a goal of 72 dpi. Assuming you really want assistance with this, you can utilize a picture resizer apparatus.

Do whatever it takes not to mess your picture since it will be somewhat little. Likewise, consider making a logo for the cover to make it effectively unique. To additional assistance with your plan, you can utilize stock pictures, webcast cover formats from Canva or recruit an expert from Fiverr. Look at probably the best digital broadcast logos for incentive to assist you with beginning.

12. Welcome webcast visitors

Welcoming visitors to your webcast can make your show more conversational, permitting an external voice to be heard. Visitors can offer one of a kind viewpoints and feature information that can be profoundly important to your digital broadcast's subject. Individuals to incorporate as visitors can be companions, family, collaborators or pioneers in your industry. To welcome visitors to your show, you can connect with them straightforwardly. Virtual entertainment destinations, including LinkedIn, can be an incredible spot to find or message high-profile visitors. In any case, keep an eye on a competitor's resume site for a telephone number or email to reach them.

Recording and Altering

13. Track down a spot to record

Not all podcasting spaces are made similarly. The best setting to record your digital broadcast is a tranquil spot, in a perfect world with materials that can retain sound. Instances of such things you need close by are: shelves, garments, love seats and covers. Assuming that you end up having a stroll in storage room, that could be an optimal area to record. When you're prepared, you can stir up to a recording studio with soundproofing materials like froth boards for the best quality

14. Utilize the right amplifier strategies

To save time when altering your substance, guarantee that you record yourself in the most effective way conceivable by carrying out great amplifier strategies all along. Follow these prescribed procedures while involving a mouthpiece for your digital broadcast:

- Position your receiver five to six inches (or five fingers) away from your mouth.

- Slant your mic at 45 degrees for your voice to get caught in the greatest.

- Create some distance from the amplifier when you're not addressing keep away from superfluous recording commotions.

15. Record distant visitors or co-hosts

To record distant visitors, you can utilize programming like Skype, Zoom, SquadCast, Alitu and Zencastr. Moreover, Anchor is an incredible free instrument that can interface you with up to ten individuals so you can record together from anyplace. With this device, individuals can record themselves straightforwardly from their telephones, so you won't have to request that your visitors put resources into a receiver. There is even a capacity called "Anchor Co-has" that matches you up with an outsider keen on examining comparative themes. Regardless, when you save the record from your meeting, you can alter everything in one spot.

16. Work with altering programming

Digital broadcast recording and altering programming permit you to tidy up your sound from commotions, cut portions, layer on music and move around various areas. The absolute most popular altering programming are: Alitu, Anchor, Daringness and Adobe Tryout. Notwithstanding, there are something else to browse.

Editing tips:

- Make a layout in which your introductions, outros and promotion openings are secured, so you simply have to include your voice for that day's episode.

- First alter for content, then interruptions. Zeroing in on each in turn will make the cycle faster.

- In your settings, add compressions to make your voice sound more alleviating and allow innovation to mechanize commotion evacuation.

- Utilize sound blurs between tracks for smooth-sounding advances.

- While trading, consider adding ID3 tags so your media player has the right data about your episode.• If by some stroke of good luck your voice is recorded, set the bitrates to 96 kbps, and assuming you likewise have music, set it to 192 kbps. This will clean your voice and make it more alleviating.

Launching

17. Pick a webcast Hosting Site

Not every person knows about this, yet digital recording registries, for example, Apple Webcasts and Spotify don't permit you to straightforwardly transfer episodes to their foundation. All things considered, you should pick a digital recording facilitating site that stores and broadcasts your sound documents. This site then creates a RSS channel for you that gets imparted to indexes.

At the point when you start a web recording, survey the best digital broadcast facilitating locales to pick the stage you really want. We assembled 15 stages in view of highlights, cost, capacity, examination and appropriation mixes. Here are the best five:

- Podbean (has a free plan)

The Ultimate Guide

- Buzzsprout (free for 90 days)

- Libsyn

- Spreaker (has a free plan)

- Simplecast

18. Make a site for your webcast

On top of displaying your webcast episodes, making a site permits you to share foundation data about yourself and different hosts. A site likewise gives a consistent method for acquiring new business valuable open doors, since potential teammates can undoubtedly reach out. Regardless of which podcasting host you have, the Wix Webcast Player transfers your substance onto your site by pulling its RSS channel URL. To assist you with sending off, we've made free digital recording site formats that as of now have the webcast player underlying and are planned considering tuning in. Young lady, You're Recruited: New employee screening Tips is a digital recording site model based on Wix. The maker additionally involved the Wix Logo Producer for the digital broadcast symbol.

Likewise, by adding a free blog and setting your digital broadcast one next to the other, you can acquire Search engine optimization traffic and adapt your show, which we'll examine later. You can likewise add a contact structure to gather supporters' email addresses for future email showcasing efforts and illuminate them to tune in for new episodes, occasions and offer other energizing news.

19. Compose a portrayal for your web recording

Very much like we read the rear of a book cover prior to choosing to buy it, audience members most frequently judge a web recording by its portrayal. In this manner, ensure your outline is extremely captivating and distinct. To do this, cover the accompanying focuses:

- What your identity is

- Who this digital broadcast is for

- What the audience will get o

For example, Karin Ronin's webcast portrayal effectively verbalizes that her digital recording is for pioneers who need to fabricate their perceivability and impact. Karin likewise presents her name and tells individuals that they can anticipate that she should share systems, bits of knowledge, and question and answer episodes around initiative advancement every week.

20. Title your episodes

Webcast registries work in much the same way to web crawlers as they show applicable shows in view of catchphrases entered. Along these lines, your episode titles ought to be distinct and accessible. Do catchphrase exploration to comprehend which classifications you need your digital recording to fall under and which expressions match the searcher's expectation.

Besides, expect to compose titles that feature the episode's worth and what the audience members will get from it, for example, "X Tips For..." or "How to... " Investigate how Pete Mockaitis utilizes an episode title design that both distinguishes a center inquiry and addresses the benefit of tuning in. Here are straightforward models: "How to Come to Your Meaningful conclusion and Impart like a Pioneer" and "How to Develop Your Profession Quicker through Perusing."

21. Present your show to digital broadcast registries

When you have three to five episodes recorded, altered and transferred to your webcast facilitating webpage, now is the ideal time to distribute and impart it to the world. You will actually want to present your show with your RSS channel URL, which is tracked down in the dashboard of your webcast facilitating webpage. There's a high opportunity your digital recording facilitating administration has an immediate connection to present your webcast utilizing their device, so attempt that choice prior to going the manual course framed underneath.

The most widely recognized webcast registries to begin submitting to are Spotify and Apple podcast. In any case, there are north of 40 web recording catalogs you ought to consider growing to amplify reach.

How to present your digital recor podcast to Spotify

1. Log in to Spotify for Podcasters with your Spotify account, or pick Join to make one.

2. Click begin

3. Paste in the connection to your webcast's RSS channel.

4. Spotify will send a check email. Duplicate the code from that email and paste in the submit form.

5. Add your web recording data like the class, language, and nation and press submit.

How to present your podcast to Apple Digital broadcasts

1. In Apple Digital broadcasts Interface, click the Add button and select New Show.

2. Choose "Add a show with a RSS channel, enter the RSS channel URL and snap Save.

3. Review your show subtleties on the Show Data page to guarantee all that looks right.

4. Provide contact data for the show.

5. Set the Substance Privileges and affirm that your show has freedoms to any outsider substance it might contain and present your show for survey.

Promoting and becoming your web recording

22. Execute a podcast showcasing technique

The normal digital broadcast gets around 27 listens per episode. Interestingly, the top 1% of webcasts get around 3,200 listens per episode. Where on this range do you expect to fall? In the event that you're hoping to develop your crowd to a gigantic scope, it's pivotal to expand the manners by which individuals can find your web recording. The most well-known ways digital broadcasts are found are through graphs and proposals on listening applications and informal. Be that as it may, there are numerous other advertising techniques to remember for your webcast development procedure:

• Share via Social media: Offer your episodes across various web-based entertainment channels utilized by your main interest group. Make mystery recordings, records or other solid online entertainment designs to give sneak looks of your show that can create interest. Furthermore, join important discussions and gatherings around your point to turn out to be essential for the podcasting local area.

- Run email advertising efforts: Construct email records and send email showcasing efforts illuminating clients to pay attention to your freshest episodes. You might in fact run advancements and request clients to submit questions or become visitors on your show. Likewise, this sort of correspondence guarantees you're not neglected and reminds your crowd to monitor your show.

- Augment surveys and tributes: Let your fans talk you up. Then, at that point, share their astonishing surveys with others. When individuals hear extraordinary input, they'll be more inquisitive to check your show out. Make sure to request this input during your episodes.

- Welcome on visitors and be a visitor: Uncover yourself and your show to new crowds by going onto other digital recordings or carrying notable individuals to go about as visitors on yours. Along these lines, you can cross-market yourselves and extend your scope.

- Compose blog entries: Sum up what's going on with your episode and use writing for a blog Website design enhancement improvements so that you'll be seen as high up on web crawlers.

- Fiddle with paid advertisements: Browse various sorts of publicizing efforts that focus on your crowd. This can be supported online entertainment posts or even paid search advertisements.

- Network with other podcasters: It's not consistently what you know, yet who you know that is important. Go to occasions, assemble associations and get to know other podcasters who you can gain from. You can constantly ask them for exhortation on the best way to begin a digital recording.

- Contact brands and individuals you notice: In the event that you give a whoop to an individual or an item, it's likewise to their greatest advantage for whatever number individuals as could be expected under the circumstances to hear it. Send the episode their way with a well disposed note, and ideally, they'll very much love to share it.

23. Keep individuals tuning In

Most importantly, an established method for keeping individuals returning is by requesting that they buy into your podcast. Along these lines, they'll be cautioned when you discharge new happy. Furthermore, center around constantly adding esteem and drawing in with audience members. You will naturally lead individuals to partake in your show such a lot of that they'll need to hear more from you.

Ultimately, to fabricate crowd commitment and to make a feeling of local area, you can do things like take voice messages from audience members, record a fragment with a fortunate endorser or basically have back and forth discussions and take inquiries from your audience members. Envision sending an inquiry to your most loved web recording host. Couldn't you need to pay attention to the following episode to see whether they responded to it and what they said?

24. Adapt your webcast

So you dominated how to begin your webcast and have a reliable measure of audience members. Presently you can start to adapt it. A great many people bring in cash podcasting by running promotions, charging paid memberships or requesting gifts through stages like Patreon or PayPal.

If you have any desire to run promotions during your show, you can apply to collaborate with stages, for example, Midroll, Promotion Results Media and Genuine Local Media. What's more, be guaranteed, research shows 78% of audience members wouldn't fret digital recording publicizing for of supporting free happy. Fortunately, digital broadcast promotions are likewise extremely powerful. Contrasted with customary promoting, 10% more audience members are probably going to purchase after openness to web recording advertisements.

25. Distribute new happy consistently

The key to digital recording achievement is consistency. Make a timetable for your show and plan to deliver basically a couple of new episodes a month. On the off chance that it's simpler for you to mass record, you can record a full season at one time, buying yourself time until you record and distribute the following one. However long your audience members know when to expect more satisfied, they'll probably return for more.

CHAPTER NINE
SELL DIGITAL PRODUCTS ON GUMROAD

As some of you may definitely be aware, Gumroad is a web-based stage that permits its clients to sell courses and other advanced items, including *icons, emojis, C4D scenes, Procreate brush packs, comic books, cookbooks, plugins, templates, top 10 lists,* and *crypto tips.* If by chance you're a well-informed authority of any sort, you can change over your insight and experience into a significant pay by offering on the web classes to students and any other individual who needs to learn. Gumroad allows you to set up a web-based store for your advanced items on its foundation and implant it on your webpage.

Furthermore, Gumroad permits its clients to sell and get compensated quick. Gumroad highlights an adaptable page manager that assists you with building a delightful retail facade in only a couple of moments. With regards to getting installments, Gumroad permits you to make basic enrollments (your clients will approach your substance however long they're bought in), set up memberships (month to month, quarterly, yearly, and so forth), and proposition your crowd the opportunity to name their cost.

Reasons to sell advanced items on Gumroad:

• Gumroad offers a free arrangement for makers of any sort (exchange charges not considered);

• Gumroad permits you to acknowledge installments in various monetary forms, as well as PayPal and Mastercard installments;

- Gumroad allows you to make rebate codes for your items; and

- Gumroad allows you the opportunity to develop your crowd by posting refreshes, sending messages, and utilizing mechanized work processes.

Gumroad doesn't appear to be the right stage for your internet based course? No problem, there are a lot of different choices available to you. You can begin your showing process on Workable, SkillShare, Udemy, ClickBank, and JVZoo.

Method To Procure A Side Pay Selling Digital Products

An entirely different universe of potential income streams look for you and getting everything rolling is more straightforward than you naturally suspect. Truth be told, your most prominent financial additions might be the simplest you've made. A totally different universe of potential income streams look for you and beginning is simpler than you suspect. As a matter of fact, your most noteworthy money related gains might be the simplest you've made. Advanced items are gradually removing piece of the pie from their actual partners and, now and again, opening up new potential income stream open doors.

Take the music business, for instance.

Throughout the past 10 years or somewhere in the vicinity, actual Albums and tapes have missed out to their computerized partners as found in the prospering progress of stages like iTunes and Spotify. We can comprehend this all the more substantially by taking a gander at Compact disc deals in 2020 which represented just 5.5% of all out music industry income contrasted with 90% in 1999.

In the book business, digital books have significantly expanded their piece of the pie to a figure around 21% of all out book deals as of this current year. This is up from 14% in 2019 which is characteristic of its quick development. There's an example to be learned here: individuals will pay cash for comfort and quick openness. Regardless of whether the doesn't item cost anything to make (since it's advanced!).

Selling computerized items is a minimal expense, okay method for testing and begin creating different income streams. Innovation arrangements have made it simple to sell advanced items starting around 2011. Stages devoted to giving individuals the opportunity to work, learn, and live the way that they need have changed the innovative scene, abstracting away the assignments of facilitating items, dealing with installments, and figuring out deals information. As computerized dissemination and online business stages have developed throughout the last 10 years, the abilities of effective business people and makers have remained thsame: a sharp enthusiasm for what merits offering, how to sell it, and the least demanding method for getting everything rolling. Procuring a side pay from selling computerized items begins with understanding what they are and for what reason to sell them. What's more, it relies further upon imagining, approving, and driving items in interest.

What Is A Digital Product?

Digital product are anything that you can pay for and afterward download and consume immediately. At the end of the day, they are products that can be sold in a computerized structure and afterward recovered from a web-based gadget. The main things that come to the vast majority's psyches when the words 'Digital product' are utilized are the ones we as a whole know and love. I'm alluding to your most loved Arouse books or your next Netflix gorge show. Indeed, these are computerized items!

The stirring news is you must not have a billion-dollar spending plan to procure a side pay making or selling computerized items. Making a computerized item might take as much time as necessary, yet it requires no cash. We will investigate computerized items you'll have the option to deliver and sell without burning through every last cent (or your imaginative brain). Simply remember a something, on the off chance that it tends to be seen on the web, it very well may be sold on the web. You simply have to sort out how your skill can be made into a Digital product that can then be showcased to engage your interest group.

Advantages of Selling Digital Products

Before we go down the extremely persuading way regarding every one of the advantages of selling advanced items, it is vital to understand that this way can be for everybody. Well informed individuals have constructed organizations around stages that can simplify the entire interaction. Like Gumroad ;) yet to a greater degree toward that later.

You don't need to be a specialized intellectual to receive the benefits of our undeniably computerized economy, We should hop into the delicious advantages;

1. Practically zero Startup Expenses

Individuals frequently face efficient obstructions to passage: they have an extraordinary thought and need to begin selling something just to understand that they need a ton of cash-flow to get things going. The idea of advanced items implies that your beginning up costs are very low. This is potential because of the web-based commercial centers and changing internet business devices that are not difficult to utilize and remove the vast majority of the problem that individuals believe is expected to begin selling. By joining a thought with a few energy and a little concentration, you'll have the option to get your thought onto a stage and begin selling without the requirement for a credit or funding. Every one of this implies a certain something: Higher net revenues.

2. Flexibility is a Feature

Increasingly more organization groups are progressing to remote work which is perfect, however you're in many cases actually expected to be attached to your (home) work area for a set number of hours or gatherings. The incredible thing about selling advanced items is it's your own virtual business, meaning you choose how long and from where you need to chip away at it. You have full command over everything.

3. Don't bother Paying for Actual Extra room Consistently

Coordinated factors can be an ongoing sink with regards to selling items. It's not hard to envision - actual items require creation costs, actual capacity game plans, and installments, as well as possibly irksome transportation plans. Selling advanced items eliminates the need for any of this which makes it an optimal side (and full-time) hustle. Aside from being the most reduced cost items that you can sell, selling computerized items implies a less distressing life contrasted with the actual item elective.

4. The Cash Streams in Latently

When your item is set up and begins selling, there's not all that much you require doing, other than showcasing. That is the excellence of automated revenue. So regardless of whether you live it up work, procuring a side pay selling Digital product online can in any case get cash consistently. The excellence of advanced items is you're not selling time for cash, which can set you well en route to carrying on with the sort of life you like with more opportunity. In the event that one of your objectives is to create financial wellbeing, an automated source of income is one of the definite fire ways of achieving this.

5. No Roof on Procuring Potential

The more you sell advanced items, the more your net revenues increment and improve with time. The justification behind that is basic - you don't have to spend more the means to deliver more things of whatever you're selling.

Thus, selling advanced items has (nearly) limitless procuring potential. The virtual idea of what you're selling implies that you'll have the option to offer your item to anybody that has a functioning web association and an email account.

6. You are in Finished Control

Because of the disposal of superfluous calculated above like delivery, stockpiling, and assembling your item, we show up at the 6th benefit of selling computerized items - you are in finished control. You choose everything - what to make, what cost to sell it for, and where to sell it from. You can possibly offer to anybody on the planet because of the absence of any actual limitations.

Some of the Best Digital Products to Sell Online

1. **Videos and Online Courses**

Think about the last time you had an inquiry that you looked for on Google. Odds are you've considered a video to be a recommended reply. The vast majority of us love to learn new things, yet The way in which we learn it has a significant effect. Some lean toward video, some sound, and some text. Other than the notoriety of video learning, it's likewise commonly more costly than digital books or other computerized items. And that implies you can procure more $.So whether you're hoping to make a video "on the most proficient method to set up greeting pages without any preparation utilizing the most recent tech" or a series about "how to begin a workmanship profession as a fledgling", you should adapt it. A top procuring maker on Gumroad who does this well is Daniel from Cold Email Wizard. He began selling a digital book for $17 and after some time, began adding recordings to his course which presently sells for more than $200.

Digital books address one of the numerous fabulous advantages of our tech-driven life: accommodation. By making and delivering a digital book, you're giving admittance as far as anyone is concerned in a structure that can be consumed on tablets, telephones, tablets, and PCs. This implies content that your perusers can take with them anyplace. It's an ideal option for thoughtful people and it's sup

1. Open Google Docs or Microsoft Word.

2. Write the substance.

3. Design a cover on Canva.

4. Save it as a PDF.

5. Create a Gumroad account (it requires 2 minutes).

6. Publish it to Gumroad.

7. Start selling.

We have such countless astonishing makers selling digital books on Gumroad.

Adam Wathan and Steve Schoger sell a famous digital book to improve as a website specialist. Kristina Earn sells a very well known self-teaching educational program as PDF archives.

2. **Templates and Plans**

Layouts and plans are a lifeline for UI planners, craftsmen, picture takers, originators and website specialists as well. It saves such a lot of time, and when you can save time for other people, you can bring in cash from it.

Jingsketch is one of our top makers selling outlines, instructional tutorials and brushes.

Mateusz sells UI Units for Figma.

Kyle sells Tailwind layouts.

Pablo sells hand-drawn representations.

3. **Audio**

In the event that music is your obsession and you've worked in music creation, why not make executioner beats and begin selling them on the web? This could be soundtracks, tunes, circles, and, surprisingly, audio effects. Film studios, podcasters, decorations and content makers are continuously searching for new sound to use in their creations.

You as of now have the ability and expertise; why not figure out how to adapt from your enthusiasm and inventiveness so you can begin producing a side pay as well? Stunningly better, why not make a video course helping others to turn into a performer too? Mutual benefit.

Digital Product Ideas

Now that you know probably the best computerized items to sell on the web, we should dig a piece further into additional thoughts of what you can offer. That's right, there are many models, yet the following are a couple of famous guides to consider:

For the tech savvy:

- You could sell website themes, applications or other programming that can then be sold as service (SaaS).

Assuming that you're great at making sense of:

- You could make video instructional exercises, digital books or paid bulletins making sense of an interaction or expertise.

On the off chance that you're a gifted speaker:

- You could make a premium webcast individuals can buy into.

In the event that you love cooking:

- You could make a recipe book, diet plans and cooking classes.

On the off chance that you love to plan things:

- You could make PSD records, layouts, symbol packs and configuration courses.

In the event that you love photography:

- You could make light room packs and photography courses.

The focal point here is that you can earn enough to pay the bills selling a skill and love doing it as well! :)

Step by step instructions to make the Best Computerized Items

1.   Build a crowd of people

One of the most incredible ways of making a famous computerized item is to initially make a crowd of people.

This is the way Arvid Kahl began, He talked about how he grew a SaaS (Software as a Service) on his virtual entertainment channels, and he before long began getting customary inquiries on how he did this and any tips he can share. What did he do straightaway? He made an item, obviously Zero to Sold was brought into the world from his crowd spurring the interest.

Important point:

1.   Talk about what you appreciate and what you're proficient in.

2.   Then make an item founded on the interest and interest from your crowd.

3.   Refine and get to the next level

Certainly, you can pause for a moment or two and begin loosening up after your initial item and it would be a good idea for it's a gigantic festival. At the point when you're prepared from your excursion, it's critical to continue refining, improving and adding to your item range. As we said before, Daniel from Cold Email Wizard began with a digital book. He presently has different courses and his items have recently been improving. This approach isn't just really great for your clients, however it additionally prompts more deals as well.

4. Consistent deals

A few of us dislike the "deals" part, yet on the off chance that your item is useful, why not with certainty advance it and spread the news? It very well may be simple for you to send off your item, yet how would you continue to produce customary, reliable deals? That is THE issue.

Platforms to Help You Sell Digital Products Effectively

There are so many stages you can utilize, however why not cover the "embed standout here" one?

Gumroad

Gumroad is a fabulous stage since they make obviously they care about their makers. It's their way of thinking that makers have the right to get compensated for their work and their worth contribution is making it unquestionably simple to get everything rolling and to begin selling as a maker. Going through their greeting page, you'll presumably end up gesturing alongside their focuses as I wound up doing - "get away from your 9-5 work area work, remove your formal attire, end your drive, get compensated for your art." They likewise offer a lot of extraordinary highlights for somebody needing to sell their computerized items.

Let's take a look at a few

1. You're ready to modify a presentation page utilizing their developer with the choice of utilizing CSS.

2. Get admittance to information with pleasant visuals that can assist with showing you what's working for yourself and where you could improve.

3. Selling items is simple with a large group of customizations that permit you to offer precisely exact thing you need in the configuration fitting your personal preference.

4. Your clients approach what they've purchased from you the subsequent they've gotten it. Moment access implies cheerful clients.

5. If you wish to add actual items to your contribution, Gumroad makes it simple to do exactly that.

6. Gumroad handles the sales Tax and VAT.

7. Gumroad is really simple to utilize - both for you as the maker, and for your client to make a buy.

8. It's totally free to utilize Gumroad.

9. Gumroad allows you to zero in on what is important - make quality items and get compensated for your work.

Visser is a Dutch craftsman who made Workmanship With Flo, a computerized craftsmanship business offering novice and high level video instructional exercises to draw and paint. She began as a singular specialist who utilized Instagram to post the cycle she used to make a picture and not the actual picture.

She even began presenting YouTube recordings on show the most common way of making a picture until she found Gumroad. Visser's most memorable Gumroad item was a bunch of fundamental brushes intended for Multiply on iPad Genius and today, she's selling in excess of 20 items on the stage.

In the mean time, Enkamp is a karate sweetheart who likewise utilized Gumroad to proceed with his art while procuring a pay. Enkamp used to compose websites about his encounters and has drawn in other karate geeks and afterward chose to transform these publishing content to a blog abilities into composing books. Presently he is a notable worldwide instructor, public group competitor, top rated creator, and organizer behind KARATEbyJesse. He distributes instructive substance and shows workshops all over the planet. Both have now been acquiring six figures selling advanced workmanship items. This can be you, as well.

Conclusively, there are different stages you can use to sell your advanced items, and a significant number of them are incredible options in contrast to Gumroad. The best is for you to test and see which one suits your requirements better.

Everybody needs to procure automated revenue, however most believe it's unrealistic to accomplish. This is just false. Procuring a side pay selling computerized items online has never been simpler with the fabulous internet based instruments accessible to organize and sell our insight and skill. The low beginning up costs and decreased boundary to passage imply that you truly can apply the "It's smarter to fall flat than never to attempt" saying unafraid of losing everything. Who knows, regardless of whether you're somewhat effective, you'll in any case have automated revenue moving in whether or not you step into the workplace or not.

CHAPTER TEN

OTHER BUSINESS IDEAS AND INDUSTRIES THAT ARE THRIVING AND WILL THRIVE

The Coronavirus pandemic has changed the way individuals work and how employees view their work lives. Thus, there was discussion of the *"great resignation"* coming. With such countless individuals laid off or found employment elsewhere for reasons unknown, there may be more would-be business people hoping to procure a pay in their own particular manner.

There are a lot of ventures and kinds of organizations that will flourish in 2022/2023. A considerable lot of these organizations will be computerized and permit business visionaries to work from home and control their hours.

1) **Virtual events and webinars**

During the Coronavirus pandemic facilitating any web-based occasions or meeting with partners over Zoom turned into the standard. There are sure benefits to facilitating an occasion online rather than, in actuality. On account of this, facilitating virtual occasions, (for example, online classes) and gatherings have a whole industry all alone. There's certainly an opportunity that virtual occasions will remain, in any event, when things "fully recover" As we see currently.

With virtual occasions, more individuals will actually want to go to them. On the off chance that you track down a virtual occasion, assuming you live in New York, you could go to an occasion in London or Beijing. Without applications like Zoom, Microsoft Groups, etc, less individuals would go to any occasions.

The fellow benefactor of Twine, Coburn Lawrence, expressed that the participation for virtual occasions was four or five a greater number of than in-person occasions. There are work open doors for arranging, facilitating, and pulling off these virtual gatherings and occasions with high participation for virtual occasions.

2) Health and wellness

The wellbeing and health industry was at that point deeply grounded before the Coronavirus pandemic. As per McKinsey and Company, the wellbeing business was worth more than $1.5 trillion, actually becoming yet the Coronavirus pandemic changed individuals' opinion on their wellbeing and health. This change was accounted for by Bloomberg in January 2022 this year. Individuals began to key in on something beyond their "fit figure." Individuals needed to track down better approaches to remain sound and healthy while at home. The Washington Post revealed that individuals saw the upside of practicing at home.

Acumen Research and Consulting expressed that the home wellness industry will develop by 4.7% by 2027. This potential development is an expected $14.8 billion by then. This conceivable development has set out a freedom for health and wellness applications. The World Financial Gathering revealed that during the main portion of 2020, the downloading of wellbeing and wellness applications became by practically half.

There has also been a growing trend in people enjoying physical outings and activities that aren't mainly for exercise. These will include climbing, hiking, and martial arts.

3) Home Redesign And Intereior Design

In 2022, research has it that numerous Americans purchased new homes. Buying new homes prompted an extraordinary expansion in the inside plan and housing industry. In any event, when individuals haven't bought another home has helped this industry by redesigning their homes. There was an expansion in home improvement deals among May and June 2021. There are a lot of administrations that assist clients with their home redesigns and Do-It-Yourself projects.

In 2022, a Houzz and Home investigation discovered that spending on home development expanded by 15%. There was likewise an expansion in revamping open air spaces. This increment was a consequence of individuals needing to invest more time outside. There are lot of chances for you and other would-be business entrepreneurs to make an internet based stage to sell home development kit or even offer types of assistance to clients. There's the potential for giving web-based instructional exercises in inside plan and home development.

4) **Pet Care Service**

The Pandemic constrained many individuals into disconnection and additional free time. The dejection prompted more Americans taking on pets somewhat recently. As per the ASPCA, one out of five individuals took on a canine or feline dog or cat between May 2021 and May 2022. An expansion in pet adoption prompted an uncommon ascent in pet-related spending. [American Pet Products Association (APPA)](#) found that spending on pets developed from $97.1 billion to $103.6 billion in that equivalent time.

There was a radical requirement for pet care services like training, strolling, grooming, and in any event, taking care of. This need gives enough of a chance to new business people to break into the web-based pet industry. There are online stores explicitly for pets, like Tuft and

Pawand Chewy. Indeed, even internet based stages, for example, Guard dog Labs assist with petting guardians track down the best pet nourishment for their fuzzy buddies. There is even something to assist the individuals who with having lost their partners. A few sites can lead lamenting pet guardians to guiding and treatment administrations. Organizations, for example, Eterneva can produce lab-made precious stones from your late pet's remains.

5) Sustainability Items And Services

NYU stem directed statistical surveying that showed "maintainability advertised items became 7.1x quicker than items not showcased as practical." Today, more individuals know that their activities will affect the climate, which has changed their shopping designs. GWI's statistical surveying found that over half of clients needed (regardless need) reused or less bundling with their merchandise. It additionally found that 48% needed more reasonable eco-accommodating merchandise. Furthermore, 44% of clients maintained that their products should be more normal.

Entrepreneurs can offer green types of assistance on the web. For instance, digital marketing or promoting offices center around, harmless to the ecosystem businesses and the green economy. New business people can make a harmless to the ecosysem online retail business. Simply remember that new organizations overwhelmed the maintainability industry, making it challenging for clients to track down their direction. New business people can utilize this to make instructive administrations to help these clients.

6) Baby and Parenting

Another roaring web-based business area is the nurturing and child industry. The NPD found that guardians burn through huge amount of cash on products for their youngsters. In 2021, the association found that this industry produced $7.35 billion. In 2021, guardians burned through $587.5 million on wellbeing items for their youngsters. This sum was a 35% increment from 2019. These items included child furniture, toddler beds, and cribs and other wellbeing and preparing items. There was likewise an increment of 17% from 2020 ($992.1 million) in child and kid furniture deals. The hits included child furniture, baby beds, and lodgings.

Guardians additionally burned through $963.6 million on items to engage their children. These included swings and seats/jumpers.

7) Men's Beauty Products

The beauty industry has forever been a flourishing industry. The vast majority will imagine that the business' main client would be ladies. However, the business' most critical developing income comes from items focused on male clients. Allied Market Research found that the men's industry had "developed dramatically throughout the last ten years and ought to hit $226 billion by 2023."

As per a CBS News report, Mintel worldwide exploration firm found that most Gen Z men in the US need orientation free beauty product. They additionally aren't keen on items bundled in the standard manly tones. That's what the report expressed "9% of Gen Z guys say they utilize some type of lighter, 'no' cosmetics, whether it's colored lotion, BB cream or CC (colour correcting) cream."

There is a developing interest for more secure and non-harmful magnificence items. As per a Brand Substance report, the "spotless" magnificence industry is supposed to develop from $5.4 billion out of 2020 to $21.6 billion out of 2027. This pattern implies there are holes in the market that could be taken advantage of by new business visionaries. Online organizations in the magnificence business can incorporate a web-based retail location spend significant time in men's excellence and prepping items or clean excellence items.

8) **Food**

Assuming you've generally had an enthusiasm for good food yet found beginning an eatery too costly, then, at that point, I suggest that you make a food truck or phantom (virtual kitchen) business. A phantom or virtual kitchen can be considered a different kitchen that organizations utilize just for conveyance orders. While the pandemic constrained numerous eateries to close their entryways, these kitchens benefitted. Their benefit is that these kitchens can offer food conveyance and take-out administrations to clients.

An article in QSR Magazine brought up that apparition kitchens can work without the expense of being in "premium areas."

9) **Home renovation and decor**

Since the Coronavirus pandemic, more individuals have been telecommuting. More individuals working from home could have prompted the need to work on their environmental elements. As per the NPD Gathering, in 2020, laborers burned through cash to overhaul their washrooms and kitchens. The gathering likewise found that paint deals expanded by 16%, and income from home improvement deals expanded by 22%.

The expansion in deals implies that new business people can make one of a kind web-based stores or online help stages to help shoppers. Since remote work is setting down deep roots regardless of the pandemic, online stores and administrations that assist buyers in this industry will be popular for some time.

10) Toys

The toy business is one more encouraging industry for new web-based business visionaries. As per the NPD, toy retail deals have kept on developing. In 2021, toy deals produced $45.1 billion in income. A greater part of these deals were finished on the web, which became 75% between 2020 to 2021. The top-selling toys included building sets (+26%), games (+29%), design dolls and adornments (+56%), sports toys that have bikes, skateboards, and skates (+31%), and summer season toys (+24%).

The NPD has suggested that toy retailers offer a purchase on the web, pickup coming up (BOPIS), or curbside pickup choice since this would be more helpful for guardians in a rush.

(11) Coaching and Consultation

Given that you're a specialist in a specific field, training is an extraordinary method for bringing in cash on the web. This generally functions admirably assuming you first put some work into building your image online through your site. When individuals start to trust you and understand that you have skill and uprightness, they will begin to move toward you all alone. They will ask you how you got to where you are currently, how they can apply similar thoughts and strategies to their own business thoughts or organizations. From the outset, you might be enticed to offer free guidance, however as additional individuals approach you, you will want to begin charging for your interviews. Once more, how much cash you'll acquire from your meetings will rely upon the field you're in. Business mentors bring in a very decent measure of cash - somewhere near $235 each hour, and chief mentors make much more - $325 an hour

Different sorts of mentors, similar to life mentors, additionally earn substantial sums of money, yet not exactly the ones referenced above, as $160 an hour

12) Google AdSense (You'll require a site)

Google AdSense is a computerized promoting program planned by Google for bloggers, site proprietors, and YouTubers to utilize and bring in cash from the promotions publicized on Google. It's a genuinely basic system to procure pay on the web. You should join with the program and afterward Google will give you a code (known as an AdSense code) that you then need to reorder onto your site. From that point onwards, Google does the greater part of the work and you get cash each time somebody either taps on your advertisements.

Presently, the progress of your AdSense program relies upon your specialty. Normally, promotions that have to do with financial advising and insurance, as well as online instruction will bring you cash quicker than specialties like hardware, design, retail, food, wellness, and wellbeing. You can join Google AdSense for nothing. Likewise, their qualification rules are quite free, so regardless of whether you have a fresh out of the plastic new blog or webpage, you'll in any case have the option to join. Furthermore, they offer various kinds of advertisements: video, pictures and energized pictures, rich media, and text. In the event that you have a few sites, you can run the promotions from one AdSense account. If you have any desire to utilize AdSense on YouTube recordings, you'll have to have at least 1,000 suscribers and 4,000 hours of watch time.

To wrap things up, anything you do, don't cheat and tap on your own advertisements! Since Google can tell and afterward they will suspend your record endlessly. beginner-friendly and easy to get started with, the disadvantage is that the payouts are by and somewhat little. There are Google AdSense options of show promotion networks with better payouts:

• Ezoic (fledgling well disposed and suggested) is a site improvement stage for computerized distributers and site proprietors.

• Mediavine is a showcase promotion network assisting content makers with building manageable organizations. (offering the best payouts however having severe passage prerequisites. Your site needs to have somewhere around 50k meetings each month).

• AdThrive is a superior showcase promotion organization that gives total promotion streamlining administrations.

• Monumetric is a presentation promotions administration that assists distributers with monetizing their sites.

CONCLUSION

In any case, I want to believe that you had the option to find a couple of thoughts that you're willing to test. Regardless, you could basically try one of them out - you should go for it, all things considered! this permits you to enhance your pay consistently from the solace of your home. The issue right now is you end up spending cash on new methodologies that don't work out. It would be great to procure some income online without paying far too much to get everything rolling.

Obviously, I haven't depleted every one of the opportunities for bringing in cash on the web - I'd have to compose an entire book about that.

www.ingramcontent.com/pod-product-compliance
Lightning Source LLC
Chambersburg PA
CBHW031630210526
45464CB00004B/1824